D1599794

Praise for *Successful STEM Mentoring Initiatives for Underrepresented Students*

"Using research-based practices and case studies, Packard makes the case that mentoring with intention can increase college and university enrollment and graduation rates of all students in STEM—particularly women, students of color, first-generation college students, or community college transfers. She provides a critical tool that helps faculty and administrators examine their departments to identify obstacles to student's success and then implement appropriate, tested strategies, including improving everyday communications and interactions with students and teaching and advising practices. More importantly, this book is about creating an inclusive environment that makes students from all backgrounds feel like they belong in STEM."—**Yolanda S. George**, *deputy director, Education and Human Resources Programs, American Association for the Advancement of Science*

"This is a book about 'why' and 'how.' It explains why STEM student support structures, broadly defined as *mentoring*, are critical to the strength of undergraduate and graduate education in STEM fields. It explains in a clear and evidence-based narrative how individuals and departments can provide mentoring to enhance persistence of all STEM students in their respective fields, in particular those students who perceive themselves or are perceived by others as underrepresented in their fields. Packard provides guidance to help individuals and departments improve and expand their mentoring of STEM students. All STEM educators should read this book."—**David Gross**, *Department of Biochemistry & Molecular Biology, University of Massachusetts, Amherst*

"*Successful STEM Mentoring Initiatives for Underrepresented Students* illustrates and elucidates Packard's considerable expertise and scholarship on an enduring and—for some disciplines and education settings—seemingly intractable set of issues. Rather than 'tinkering around the edges' by addressing only several variables, Packard tackles underrepresentation from the perspectives of students and the education system they will encounter. This comprehensive systems approach is refreshing and, in many ways, unique. Packard offers evidence-based advice to those in higher education who are undertaking the critically important work of increasing representation of historically underserved and unserved students. She further helps readers understand where and how their roles and actions must be based on efforts that have preceded their own and how their own work will influence others in the system as students pass through it on their ways to STEM careers. It is a refreshing and much-needed approach."—**Jay B. Labov**, *senior adviser* *for education and communication, National Academies of Sciences, Engineering, and Medicine*

"Packard's book is an important resource and handbook for all academics interested in increasing the diversity of the sciences. It is a compendium of the extensive literature from social psychology, education, and other fields documenting the problems underrepresented students face and interventions that are working and also serves as a guide through that literature for those less familiar with it. Most importantly, Packard presents adaptable plans for a structured approach to effecting change at three key points in an undergraduate student's career: entry into college, declaration of a STEM major, and postgraduate planning. With this book's focus on mentoring as a relationship, there are concrete ideas here for everyone working to solve these difficult societal problems."—**Mark M. Levandoski**, *professor of chemistry, Grinnell College*

"In *Successful STEM Mentoring Initiatives for Underrepresented Students*, Becky Wai-Ling Packard addresses a longtime need of those seeking to develop more diverse and inclusive scientific and technical communities. To ensure access to useful mentoring for students approaching these communities, she provides a wonderful compendium of research-based strategies and insights that can be adapted in a wide variety of settings. I am grateful to her as a colleague and collaborator for taking the time to provide actionable advice to the many individuals in a position to provide mentoring that can improve learning, scientific discovery, innovation, technology development, and lives."—**Carol B. Muller**, *founder, MentorNet; and executive director, WISE Ventures, Stanford University*

"To our chagrin, building STEM programs that proportionally include students from historically underrepresented groups has proven to be more difficult than rocket science. Yet research and empirical evidence reveal quite clearly how to create robust STEM settings in which everyone can thrive. An award-winning scholar and educator, Packard expertly guides us through the steps of how focusing on mentoring can create and sustain inclusive STEM classrooms and departments. I have every confidence that this book will lead scientists and STEM educators to engage in empirically proven inclusive practices, one step at a time, to effect the essential changes in STEM that Packard so ably champions." —**Wendy E. Raymond**, *vice president for academic affairs and dean of faculty; professor of biology, Davidson College; former chair, National Science Foundation Committee on Equal Opportunity in Science and Engineering*

SUCCESSFUL STEM MENTORING INITIATIVES FOR UNDERREPRESENTED STUDENTS

Successful STEM Mentoring Initiatives for Underrepresented Students

A Research-Based Guide for Faculty and Administrators

Becky Wai-Ling Packard

Foreword by Norman L. Fortenberry

STERLING, VIRGINIA

Published by Stylus Publishing, LLC
22883 Quicksilver Drive
Sterling, Virginia 20166-2102

Library of Congress Cataloging-in-Publication Data
Packard, Becky Wai-Ling.
  Successful STEM mentoring initiatives for underrepresented
students : a research-based guide for faculty and administrators /
Becky Wai-Ling Packard.
    pages cm
Includes bibliographical references and index.
ISBN 978-1-62036-296-9 (pbk. : alk. paper)
ISBN 978-1-62036-295-2 (cloth : alk. paper)
ISBN 978-1-62036-297-6 (library networkable e-edition)
ISBN 978-1-62036-298-3 (consumer e-edition)
 1. Mentoring in science--United States. 2. Science--Study and
teaching (Higher)--United States. 3. Minorities in science--United
States. 4. Women in science--United States. I. Title.
Q183.3.A1P33 2015
507.1'173--dc23
                                                    2015022238
13-digit ISBN: 978-1-62036-295-2 (cloth)
13-digit ISBN: 978-1-62036-296-9 (paperback)
13-digit ISBN: 978-1-62036-297-6 (library networkable e-edition)
13-digit ISBN: 978-1-62036-298-3 (consumer e-edition)

Printed in the United States of America

All first editions printed on acid-free paper
that meets the American National Standards Institute
Z39-48 Standard.

Bulk Purchases

Quantity discounts are available for use in workshops and for
staff development.
Call 1-800-232-0223

First Edition, 2016

10   9   8   7   6   5   4

For Cian and Conall

CONTENTS

ACKNOWLEDGMENTS

I would like to thank John von Knorring and Stylus Publishing for investing in this project. I would also like to thank the administrators, faculty, staff, and students from the many institutions that have been my partners over the years for sharing their wisdom. I am grateful for the generous funding I have received for my research, and I accept all limitations in the work as my own.

I am grateful to the Summer Research Opportunity Program at the University of Michigan, where I began my inquiry, and Mount Holyoke College, where I have grown as a professional. As a first-generation college graduate and person of color, I am deeply appreciative of the many mentors who invested in my potential. Special recognition goes to Scott Paris, David Wong, P. David Pearson, Marcia Linn, and my ENGAGE in Engineering colleagues. Thank you all for believing in me and this work.

Cathy Luna, Mary Deane Sorcinelli, and Nil Santinez helped me launch this project; Rachel Hirst and Gary Gillis helped me refine my ideas. Thanks to Alyssa Dodd, Kimberly Jeffers, Rachel Maskin, Hannah Yee, and Elizabeth Auguste for their help with the final steps, and to Maureen Babineau, Minh Ly, and Lydia Peterson for their careful reading. Thanks to Amber Douglas, Kathy Foley, Sapna Thwaite, and Joan Hughes for their friendship, and to Sarah Bacon, Darby Dyar, Heather Pon-Barry, and Audrey St. John for their collaboration in this important area.

A heartfelt thank-you to Norman L. Fortenberry for his insightful foreword.

Finally, I deeply appreciate the support from my husband, Seamus, and our children.

FOREWORD

No one succeeds without assistance. There are no entirely self-made men or women. At some point someone else stood as an example, lent a hand, gave a needed piece of advice, made a well-timed introduction, or offered up a name when one was sought. These activities fall on the spectrum from passive role model to active mentor. Some individuals who have "succeeded" seem to have forgotten this objective reality. The tragedy of such forgetfulness is that those in positions of power and influence may not merely decline to provide assistance to others, they can impede the abilities of others to provide such assistance. Equally unfortunately, those who consider offering sponsorship and mentorship appropriate may preferentially do so for those with whom they feel most compatible, leaving out people with high potential but with different ways of knowing and doing.

Mentoring is important in all fields but particularly so in the science, technology, engineering, and mathematics (STEM) professions. Stereotypically, many members of these professions regard professional success as a function primarily of intellectual merit with only the most minimal role played by well-timed introductions, facilitated opportunities to showcase one's work, and invitations to key meetings and workshops. And yet, when pressed, my experience is that most STEM professionals will concede that they received valuable assistance from others throughout their careers.

For members of populations underrepresented in STEM (e.g., women of all ethnicities, persons from underserved racial and ethnic groups, persons with disabilities, etc.), purposeful and active mentoring is particularly important. This is true because while mentoring is so ubiquitous and automatic for members of dominant populations, those from underrepresented populations are often overlooked and left out. This is not necessarily pernicious. When one is part of the "in group," mentoring is offered to those members observed to have potential, connections, or simply luck. When one is part of an underrepresented population—by definition *the other*—mentoring is harder to achieve since "otherness" is a barrier to be overcome, and it is often deemed special treatment when offered. It takes effort to offer to out-group members that which is offered automatically to in-group members.

Packard offers compelling evidence on why these issues are important and provides practical guidance, based on her years of research, on how they can be successfully addressed. Critically, she advises on not only what works, but also why. Knowing "why" is crucial to understanding the extent to which a particular mentoring strategy may be applied as the circumstances and characteristics of protégés change. This book's strategy of grounding the guidance in the case studies of fictional composite characters makes the scenarios easily relatable. The incorporation of questions for readers to consider as they implement their efforts is also very helpful.

Packard's advice spans the academic landscape from pre-college students, to undergraduates, to graduate students, to faculty. In addition to providing guidance to individuals, she offers advice to academic departments as well. She provides guidance on assessing and enhancing the departmental climate in support of mentoring and accessing resources that might be available from national organizations. She suggests how mentoring can be integrated into the academic core of a department's courses, cocurricular activities, and faculty hiring, retention, and promotion practices.

This book provides a complete package. As a former faculty member, former official of the National Science Foundation's education directorate, former executive director of the National Consortium for Graduate Degrees for Minorities in Engineering and Science, Inc. (the National GEM Consortium), former director of a center for translation of education research to improved educational practice, and as a current executive director of the American Society for Engineering Education, I see this book as a key resource that would have served me well, professionally and personally, at each stage of my career. I believe this book will be immensely useful to faculty, department chairs, deans, and academic staff. More than simply a resource for individuals, this volume will provide a useful basis for workshops and seminars. It is a wonderful achievement.

Norman L. Fortenberry, ScD
Executive Director
American Society for Engineering Education

INTRODUCTION

Bill Gomez is a computer science professor at a large state research university. Every year he leads a summer program for students who have completed their first year of college. After consistently seeing very few women enroll in the summer program, he wants to improve recruitment by changing his strategy. How can Bill restructure the program to attract more women students to study computer science during their transition to college?

Susan Mason, a chemistry professor who teaches at a private liberal arts college, has noticed that many students of color take Chemistry 1, but they do not continue on to Chemistry 2, the gateway course to a chemistry major. How can Susan design a mentoring initiative to help students of color proceed successfully through this gateway into the major?

Mark Sanderson, a science, technology, engineering, and mathematics (STEM) dean at a state university's branch campus, wants to help community college transfer students succeed; many of them are also first-generation college students and would benefit from more intensive professional mentoring as they enter the job market. What kind of mentoring elements should Mark include?

As with many faculty and administrators in STEM fields, you may find yourself designing an initiative to improve the mentoring of college students.[1] Perhaps you are applying for a federal research grant and want to include a compelling section about how your work will broaden the participation of STEM students. Your focus may be on finding new ways you or your department colleagues can play a more active role in supporting persistence in STEM fields of underrepresented students, including women, students of color, first-generation college students, or community college transfer students.[2]

Despite having experience with teaching, conducting research, and advising in your field, you may not be acquainted with research-based best practices that contribute to student persistence in STEM fields, including ways to improve access to mentoring practices. *Mentoring* is a broad concept, a term that refers to many different kinds of relationships, programs, and initiatives.

Studies about mentoring are scattered across various bodies of literature, making an effective synthesis difficult to quickly generate. The reality is that those of us who are in the position to design mentoring initiatives cannot possibly share the lived experiences of all our students. We can, however, learn about the issues students face, and we can improve the ways in which we design, implement, and sustain mentoring initiatives in our departments and institutions.

The focus of my research is the mentoring and persistence of underrepresented students in STEM fields, and I often consult with faculty in STEM departments who are trying to design effective mentoring initiatives. Although Bill, Susan, and Mark are fictional composite characters in this book, their situations are representative of the wide range of cases on which I have been consulted. My interest in this work was sparked years ago when I participated in a summer science research program. In that project, my faculty mentor and I worked with staff at our local science museum on an initiative designed to foster interest in science among school-age students.[3] My participation was a life-changing experience. I went on to earn my doctorate, win grants to support my research, and I am a recipient of the Presidential Early Career Award for Scientists and Engineers. As I identify as both a first-generation college graduate and a person of color, my commitment to mentoring is deeply personal, and my recommendations are informed by years of research and practice.

I understand that as a faculty member or administrator, time is precious; you probably do not have time to sift through the literature on mentoring diverse students or cold-call other institutions to find out about the nuances of their programs. That is why I wrote *Successful STEM Mentoring Initiatives for Underrepresented Students: A Research-Based Guide for Faculty and Administrators*. This book is written for you. It is intended to guide the mentoring design process for you and your colleagues in departments of science and engineering in colleges and universities, help you recognize obstacles students may face, encourage you to consider a variety of promising mentoring approaches, and troubleshootpotential pitfalls in communication. Before going into the contents of the book, let's review why it's worth spending the time learning more about mentoring and persistence of underrepresented students in STEM fields.

Why Do We Need to Recruit Students Into STEM and Help Them Persist?

According to the National Science Board, the nation faces significant challenges in recruiting and retaining a diverse domestic and global workforce.[4] Women, first-generation college graduates, and people of color, among others, are not working in STEM careers in numbers comparable to their presence in the workforce.[5] African Americans earn 7% of bachelor's degrees in STEM.[6] Women earn fewer than 25% of bachelor's degrees awarded each year for engineering and computer science.[7] This is unfortunate because the largest projected growth in employment is happening in STEM fields, and these careers require at least a bachelor's degree.[8] Business leaders, educators, and governmental officials are united in their concern about these statistics.[9]

Persistence in STEM is often described using the metaphor of a leaky pipeline; that is, the number of potential members of the STEM workforce gradually declines because of the many "leaks" throughout K–12 education, college, and in the workforce.[10] Only about 30% of students who enter college intend to major in science or engineering, and fewer than 50% of these students complete that intended STEM major.[11] What's more, only 26% of STEM graduates are working in STEM careers.[12] Some leave STEM after earning their PhD.[13] Thus, while the opportunities in STEM are numerous, we do not see many students persisting.

Women and people of color are more likely to leave STEM fields than men or White students.[14] Community college students are also more likely to leave STEM fields before receiving an associate's degree. According to a study in Ohio, only 15% of entering community college students aspired to a STEM major, and only 15% of those original students earned an associate's degree.[15] Only 5% of the associate's degrees earned nationwide by women each year are in STEM.[16] Community college students are more likely to be of nontraditional age, students of color, working while going to school, and women.[17] You may not realize that STEM transfer students, particularly women and people of color, who arrive in four-year college or university classrooms have beaten tremendous odds to get there.

During the educational process, it is natural, of course, for some students to leave STEM fields as they engage in course work and learn more about a range of possibilities; some come to realize they are more interested in another field.[18] However, students leave STEM fields for many reasons.[19] These include a lack of information about STEM careers, limited opportunities to participate in research or other career-relevant activities, STEM courses that seem irrelevant to the world's problems, or a chilly climate in departments and workplaces for people from their social identity group.[20] Research shows that many college students who opt out of STEM are exactly the talented and capable students we'd like to keep.[21]

While the metaphor of the leaky pipeline is helpful in understanding persistence in STEM, it only takes us so far. A leaky pipeline implies that we start with a finite number of interested and capable college students and lose them over time. We need to imagine multiple paths leading *into* STEM fields.[22] Currently, about one in five people in a STEM career majored in a field other than STEM.[23] Although that's encouraging, we can do more to create on-ramps into the field.[24] Our departments can play an active role by recruiting students as they make the transition into, throughout, and even after completing college. Throughout this book, I provide examples of ways to create on-ramps into STEM and ways to support students who are already on the road to STEM careers.

Why Is Diversity in STEM Valuable?

Why is there value in diversifying the students in your classrooms? It has been argued that science-related fields have historically operated from a standpoint of selectivity and exclusion.[25] This selective exclusion is best exhibited by the strongly held practice of trying to weed out struggling students.[26] It is now accepted that this practice is pedagogically unsound, and educators have shifted away from it, recognizing that diversity and excellence *can* coexist. The term *inclusive excellence* refers to simultaneously keeping high standards while supporting students from diverse backgrounds and prior experiences.[27] Three complementary perspectives—human capital, innovation, and funding—help make the case for the benefits of diversity, particularly in our STEM classrooms.

When certain groups in our population are not represented in STEM, we are missing out on the contributions of that human capital. In the United States, we cannot expect to compete on a global scale while tapping only a small percentage of students.[28] We know, for example, that few women participate in computer science despite making strides in higher education in general; therefore, we are not involving as many people from our population in computer science as possible.[29]

From an innovation perspective, our society loses out when STEM fields do not draw together people from diverse backgrounds, whether from different lived experiences, with varied cognitive assets, or from diverse disciplines.[30] Diversely composed teams generate more creative and compelling results than more homogenously composed teams.[31] More complex thinking can result from cross-race interactions.[32] The classroom, for example, can promote rich interactions and learning among diverse students.[33]

Funding is also a compelling reason to invest in diversity. The federal government has linked STEM funding opportunities to increasing the diversity of students who pursue STEM careers. For example, National Science Foundation grant applicants must discuss how their projects broaden participation of underrepresented groups by providing outreach, teaching, or training experiences for underrepresented students. Although various grant-funding agencies may use the term *underrepresented* to indicate different groups of students, they share the goal of increasing the persistence of all STEM students and graduates.[34] The National Institutes of Health's grant programs seek to support *racial/ethnic minorities* in science (defined as Latinos/Hispanic, African American, Native American/Pacific Islanders) as well as students from economically disadvantaged or first-generation backgrounds and students with disabilities. The National Science Foundation's Louis Stokes Alliance for Minority Participation program has broadened its conception of underrepresented groups to include first-generation college and community college students. Knowing more about the experiences of students from diverse backgrounds and about mentoring can help you develop better descriptions of mentoring and persistence when designing initiatives or writing grant proposals to fund them.

Why Is Mentoring a Worthy Investment for STEM Departments?

Mentoring programs are ubiquitous. Many federal grant programs require them but if the programs are designed and implemented well, they *work*. When students have positive mentoring experiences, they are more apt to achieve better grades and persist in college.[35] Furthermore, mentoring is a high-impact educational practice, which means that your institution can expect to see increased engagement and retention as a result of your investment.[36] Underrepresented students,[37] including students from low-income backgrounds, particularly benefit from mentoring initiatives.[38] Mentoring experiences contribute positively to persistence in STEM fields.[39]

In this book, I define *mentoring* as a developmental experience or a type of support intended to advance students toward an important goal.[40] Mentoring interactions have an impact when they communicate messages of invitation or inclusion *and* equip students to take on the challenges in STEM by increasing their capabilities. To have an impact, you will need to go beyond traditional mentoring programs, which are often beneficial but can be limited in their scope, and infuse mentoring into your learning environment through the core practices of teaching and advising.[41] You will also want to try to improve the overall departmental climate.

Moreover, being able to develop and articulate a multipronged mentoring strategy is one way to invest in student success while communicating that investment to diverse prospective students and their families. When enrollment and graduation rates are used to measure success and allocate resources such as faculty lines and staff support, administrators of institutions are paying more attention than ever to mentoring as a critical investment. New faculty on the job market, and not just those from underrepresented groups, are attracted to workplace environments that emphasize inclusivity and the ability for them to thrive.[42]

What Will You Gain From This Book?

For this book I have assembled key research-based explanations about why underrepresented college students face obstacles in STEM fields and how to translate those obstacles into mentoring opportunities. Start by mapping the landscape of factors so you can see the big picture of student persistence. Then choose a focus and identify where your efforts could have the biggest impact. By looking broadly at the different kinds of mentoring approaches, you can develop a strategy to achieve your goals. And by taking an inventory of the mentoring initiatives you already have, you can try to use your existing resources where possible.

I then describe many excellent approaches being implemented on several campuses, illustrate each approach, and explain why the approach works to improve recruitment and persistence in STEM. My discussion focuses on each of the three key transitions in college: the transition into college, the transition into the major, and the transition into the workplace or graduate school. These transitions are critical times when mentoring initiatives can invite more underrepresented students into STEM departments as well as facilitate their persistence in a field. For each transition, a different case scenario—Bill's, Susan's, or Mark's situation—illustrates the mentoring design process, from consulting your own data sources to clarifying obstacles to developing a mentoring strategy to creating a plan to pilot your efforts and track your progress.

In the final section, I focus on the nuances of communication in mentoring, which influence the impact you will have. At the individual level, I articulate effective ways to frame difficult mentoring messages to students (e.g., providing constructive feedback about a student's poor performance). At the departmental level, I provide conversation starters to engage your colleagues in discussions about departmental climate. Whether you embark on a collective curricular project or examine your hiring practices, you will identify steps you can take toward a more inclusive department.

It is important for you to take a step forward wherever you are and with whatever resources you have. The scope of the challenge is large, and yet small changes can tip the balance for your department, making a powerful difference for students and for ourselves. Let's get started. One student, one colleague, one interaction at a time.

Reader Questions

- What do I already know about STEM recruitment and persistence? What questions do I have?
- What ideas do I already have about mentoring, based on my own experiences as a student and in my current role?
- How might my experiences in STEM departments and in mentoring be similar or different from those of underrepresented students? From those of my colleagues?
- What's unique about my institution, my department, or my field? How might that play a role in the challenges we face in regard to diversity? How might the unique characteristics influence what works?
- What other questions or ideas do I have?

Notes

1. The definition of *STEM* can vary, but in this volume it refers to any field in science, technology, engineering, or math. Note, however, that biological science and electrical engineering, for example, are distinct fields of study and have their own norms, resources, and barriers.

2. *Persistence* is the term used in this book to capture the experiences of students as they continue their pursuit of STEM. *Retention* typically refers to persistence initiatives from the standpoint of the institution.

3. Paris, S. G, Yambor, K. M., & Packard, B. W. (1998). Hands-on biology: A museum-schools-university partnership for enhancing students' interest and learning in science. *Elementary School Journal, 98*(3), 267–288.

4. National Science Board. (2012). *Science and engineering indicators 2012.* Retrieved from www.nsf.gov/statistics/seind12/c3/c3h.htm

5. National Science Foundation. (2007). *Women, minorities, and persons with disabilities in science and engineering.* Retrieved from ERIC database. (ED496396)

6. Landivar, L. C. (2013). *Disparities in STEM employment by sex, race, and Hispanic origin* (American Community Survey Reports, ACS-24). Retrieved from www.census.gov/prod/2013pubs/acs-24.pdf

7. Yoder, B. L. (2011). *Engineering by the numbers.* Retrieved from www.asee .org/papers-and-publications/publications/college-profiles/2011-profile-engineering-statistics.pdf

8. Carnevale, A. P., Smith, N., & Strohl, J. (2010). *Help wanted: Projections of jobs and education requirements through 2018.* Retrieved from ERIC database. (ED524311)

9. To learn about one initiative involving business leaders, educators, and government officials, see White House. (September 16, 2010). *Remarks by the president at the announcement of the "Change the Equation Initiative."* Retrieved from www.whitehouse.gov/the-press-office/2010/09/16/remarks-president-announcement-change-equation-initiative

10. Preston, A. E. (2004). Plugging the leaks in the scientific workforce. *Issues in Science & Technology, 20*(4), 69–74.

11. Higher Education Research Institute. (2010). *Degrees of success: Bachelor's degree completion rates among initial STEM majors.* Los Angeles, LA: Author.

12. Landivar, L. C. (2013). *The relationship between science and engineering education and employment in STEM occupations* (American Community Survey Reports, ACS-23). Retrieved from www.census.gov/prod/2013pubs/acs-23.pdf

13. Turk-Bicakci, L., Berger, A., & Haxton, C. (2014). *Leaving STEM: STEM Ph.D. holders in non STEM careers.* Retrieved from www.air.org/sites/default/files/downloads/report/STEM%20nonacademic%20careers%20April14.pdf

14. Seymour, E., & Hewitt, N. (1997). *Talking about leaving: Why undergraduates leave the sciences.* Boulder, CO: Westview Press.

15. Bettinger, E. P. (2010). To be or not to be: Major choices in budding scientists. In C. Clotfelter (Ed.), *American universities in a global market* (pp. 69–98). Chicago, IL: University of Chicago Press.

16. Hardy, D. E., & Katsinas, S. G. (2010). Changing STEM associate's degree production in public associate's colleges from 1985 to 2005: Exploring institutional type, gender and field of study. *Journal of Women and Minorities in Science and Engineering, 16*(1), 7–32.

17. Packard, B. W., Gagnon, J. L., LaBelle, O., Jeffers, K., & Lynn, E. (2011). Women's experiences in the STEM community college transfer pathway. *Journal of Women and Minorities in Science and Engineering, 17*(2), 129–147.

18. Thoman, D. B., Arizaga, J. A., Smith, J. L., Story, T. S., & Soncuya, G. (2014). The grass is greener in non-science, technology, engineering, and math classes: Examining the role of competing belonging to undergraduate women's vulnerability to being pulled away from science. *Psychology of Women Quarterly, 38*(2), 246–258.

19. Hewlett, S. A., Luce, C. B., Servon, L. J., Sherbin, L., Shiller, P., Sosnovich, E., & Sumberg, K. (2008). The Athena factor: Reversing the brain drain in science, engineering, and technology. *Harvard Business Review, 88*, 1–100.

20. Graham, M. J., Frederick, J., Byars-Winston, A., Hunter, A., & Handelsman, J. (2013). Increasing persistence of college students in STEM. *Science, 341*(6153), 1455–1456.

21. National Academy of Sciences, National Academy of Engineering, & Institute of Medicine. (2007). *Rising above the gathering storm: Energizing and employing America for a brighter economic future.* Washington, DC: National Academies Press.

22. Cannady, M. A., Greenwald, E., & Harris, K. N. (2014). Problematizing the STEM pipeline metaphor: Is the STEM pipeline metaphor serving our students and the STEM workforce? *Science Education, 98*(3), 443–460.

23. Landivar, L. C. (2013). *The relationship between science and engineering education and employment in STEM occupations* (American Community Survey Reports, ACS-23). Retrieved from www.census.gov/prod/2013pubs/acs-23.pdf

24. Hewlett, S. A., & Luce, S. B. (2005, March). Off-ramps and on-ramps: Keeping talented women on the road to success. *Harvard Business Review, 83*(3). Retrieved from hbr.org/2005/03/off-ramps-and-on-ramps-keeping-talented-women-on-the-road-to-success

25. Carlone, H. B. (2004). The cultural production of science in reform-based physics: Girls' access, participation, and resistance. *Journal of Research in Science Teaching, 41*(4), 392–414.

26. Seymour, E., & Hewitt, N. M. (1997). *Talking about leaving: Why undergraduates leave the sciences.* Boulder, CO: Westview Press.

27. Williams, D. A (2007). Achieving inclusive excellence: Strategies for creating real and sustained change in quality and diversity. *About Campus, 12*(1), 8–14.

28. Ong, M., Wright, C., Espinosa, L., & Orfield, G. (2011). A synthesis of empirical research on undergraduate and graduate women of color in science, technology, engineering, and mathematics. *Harvard Educational Review, 81*(2), 172–209.

29. Handelsman, J., Cantor, N., Carnes, M., Denton, D., Fine, E., Grosz, B., . . . Sheridan, J. (2005). More women in science. *Science, 309*(5738), 1190–1191.

30. Alger, J. R. (1997). The educational value of diversity. *Academe, 83*(1), 20–23.

31. Page, S. (2007). *The difference: How the power of diversity creates better groups, firms, schools and societies.* Princeton, NJ: Princeton University Press.

32. Antonio, A. L., Chang, M. J., Hakuta, K., Kenny, D. A., Levin, S., & Milem, J. F. (2004). Effects of racial diversity on complex thinking in college students. *Psychological Science, 15*(8), 507–510.

33. Terenzini, P. T., Cabrera, A. F., Colbeck, C. L., Bjorklund, S. A., & Parente, J. M. (2001). Racial and ethnic diversity in the classroom: Does it promote student learning? *Journal of Higher Education, 72*(5), 509–531.

34. In this book I focus on women, first-generation college students, low-income students, and students of color. I recognize many distinguish between underrepresented minority groups (e.g., African American, Latino, and Native American) and students of color (which can include Asian Americans or international students). I also recognize that not all underrepresented groups or students of color shared lived experiences within or across groups.

35. Crisp, G., & Cruz, I. (2009). Mentoring college students: A critical review of the literature between 1990 and 2007. *Research in Higher Education, 50*(6), 525–545.

36. Kuh, G. D. (2008). *High impact educational practices: What they are, who has access to them, and why they matter.* Washington, DC: American Association for Colleges & Universities.

37. Stolle-McAllister, K., Sto Domingo, M. R., & Carrillo, A. (2011). The Meyerhoff way: How the Meyerhoff scholarship program helps Black students succeed in the sciences. *Journal of Science Education and Technology, 20*(1), 5–16.

38. Myers, C. B., Brown, D. E., & Pavel, D. (2010). Increasing access to higher education among low-income students: The Washington State Achievers Program. *Journal of Education for Students Placed at Risk, 15*(4), 299–321.

39. Packard, B. W. (2004–2005). Mentoring and retention in college science: Reflections on the sophomore year. *Journal of College Student Retention: Research, Theory, & Practice, 6*(3), 289–300.

40. Kram, K. E. (1988). *Mentoring at work: Developmental relationships in organizational life*. Lanham, MD: University Press of America.

41. Baker, V. L., & Griffin, K. A. (2010). Beyond mentoring and advising: Toward understanding the role of faculty "developers" in student success. *About Campus, 14*(6), 2–8. doi:10.1002/abc.20002

42. See, for example, Alger, J. R., Chapa, J., Gudeman, R. H., Marin, P., Maruyama, G., Milem, J. F., . . . Wilds, D. J. (2000). *Does diversity make a difference? Three research studies on diversity in college classrooms*. Washington, DC: American Council on Education and American Association of University Professors. Retrieved from www.aaup.org/NR/rdonlyres/97003B7B-055F-4318-B14A-5336321FB742/0/DIVREP.PDF

1

MAP THE LANDSCAPE, CHOOSE A FOCUS

In this chapter, I focus on how capacity, interest, and belongingness influence student persistence in STEM. I provide a map of the landscape to illustrate how these factors operate in the individual, the learning environment, and the departmental climate. Although seeing the big picture is important, so is finding a manageable focus for your efforts. You might investigate how one of these factors manifests itself in the classroom environment or how another has an impact on STEM persistence during any key transition during college. At the end of the chapter, you are asked to reflect on your own department and the information you can use to map your landscape and choose your focus.

Map the Landscape Using the Ecological Model

An ecological model can help us create a map of the environmental landscape and visualize the big picture with regard to how various factors influence the persistence of STEM students.[1] According to the ecological model, learning and development occur within a set of nested, interconnected contexts. Some factors have a more direct influence on individuals because they are present in the immediate environment. Other factors influence individuals indirectly, such as available resources or policies that affect the qualities of the immediate environment.

Let's illustrate using an example, possibly familiar to those working in STEM fields. Imagine you find out that a particular type of bird thrives in one environment, but when introduced to another environment, that same type of bird does not fare well. To understand why, you might start by examining a sample of birds for indicators of their physical health such as weight and heart rate. You would likely compare the features of the environment

11

where the birds thrive to those of the other environment where the birds do not. For example, you might take water samples from the local river, a place the birds are known to frequent. Because the quality of water from the river and the food supply are affected by the concentration of factories or other contributors of pollution in close proximity, the policies that govern the disposal of contaminants may be important to your inquiry. It is unlikely that one would develop an intervention to simply target the birds in decline by, say, providing food through a special program without also taking into account how pollution is affecting the water or how policies that restrict fishing affect the food supply.

When trying to understand the persistence of students in STEM, we similarly want to see the big picture, or the ecosystem.[2] We want to identify factors that influence students, including the prior knowledge that students bring with them as well as factors in the learning environment and in the broader climate that indirectly shape students' experiences. Just as birds thrive in some environments but not in others, sometimes students experience a learning environment or departmental climate that introduces an obstacle or intensifies an existing challenge. For example, a student may lack a particular requisite skill for a specific course, or a gateway course may not be structured to provide regular, timely feedback, which impedes the student's development of problem-solving skills. Resources may be scarce, affecting the ability for instructors to provide timely feedback: Perhaps class sizes are very large, or instructors have not built in opportunities to test learning formatively. Also, a gateway course that has a reputation for trying to weed out students may deter students from enrolling in it and, ultimately, deter students from the major.[3]

Primary Factors Influencing Persistence: Obstacles and Opportunities

I organize the primary factors that influence students' persistence in STEM into three broad categories: capacity, interest, and belongingness. I explain each of these factors, analyzing how they influence students. I show how the factors contribute to creating obstacles in student experiences and then translate into opportunities for mentoring initiatives.

Capacity

The capacity to learn and demonstrate competence in STEM is the factor most commonly studied when trying to understand persistence. Capacity is sometimes measured by the student's ability, aptitude, competency, performance, or evidence of skill development. When students demonstrate capacity to successfully complete the work of STEM, they are more likely to persist in STEM fields.[4] The primary indicator of having the capacity to learn is student performance in courses. However, performance is often assessed through multiple-choice exams that may not accurately reflect what students can do or what they know.[5] Special learning experiences, such as summer research programs, are often reserved for students who have already demonstrated they are capable, when in fact these very experiences provide opportunities for deepening understanding in courses and increasing capability in STEM problem-solving skills.[6]

Unfortunately, there is still a widespread belief that math and science abilities are preordained and fixed, and that no amount of excellent teaching will help increase students' abilities.[7] If one sees ability as fixed rather than malleable, then there is no role for remediation. However, years of research have demonstrated that ability can grow and change.[8] Embracing Dweck's work on *growth mind-set*, or the belief that individuals can increase their abilities, can have a powerful influence on the strategies a person uses for skill development.[9] *Fixed mind-sets*, in contrast, hold students back from trying new strategies or practicing their skills and deter instructors from working effectively with students in ways that will improve their competencies.[10] Students may discover in a gateway course that they lack the requisite skills, but their institution does not have any way to provide prerequisite modules such as programs that boost understanding of spatial relations, precalculus, or some other developmental course work.[11]

Self-efficacy, or confidence in one's ability to achieve, is often more predictive of performance than actual ability.[12] This is why it is important to equip students with opportunities to build their confidence as well as their actual competence in STEM, whether by scaffolding complex math problems so that students internalize their progress or providing opportunities to experiment with research methods and equipment in science labs to increase their familiarity with these tools.[13] The reasoning of experts in the field often does not resemble that of novice students, creating a challenge for expert teachers as they design supports for student learning because they may not be in touch with the misconceptions or stumbling blocks some students face.[14]

Unfortunately, students, particularly underrepresented students, tend to have less-than-ideal experiences in their gateway courses.[15] Gateway courses are often designed to weed out struggling students from STEM rather than develop students' emergent capacities.[16] Even the strongest students' self-efficacy can be shaken if they do not receive timely, effective feedback necessary to understand their performance and improve their competence in STEM.[17] When students learn alone in class or study in isolation outside class, they miss out on chances to engage actively with material, debate with peers, and deepen their comprehension.[18]

It is important to note that courses are taught in a social world where stereotypes about underrepresented students and their potential capability exist.[19] When students are made aware of negative stereotypes about their own demographic group, they are more likely to face *stereotype threat*, in which students underperform in high-stress situations regardless of their actual capacity to complete the work.[20] In fact, being asked simply to indicate one's gender or race on a form before taking a test can activate a negative stereotype and diminish performance. An example of this is seen in White men when they are aware of the stereotype regarding the superiority of Asian men in math.[21] Many underrepresented students, including women, first-generation college students, and students of color, underperform in gateway courses.[22] We need to acknowledge that stereotypes and social dynamics play some role in these students' participation and learning.[23]

Mentoring opportunities to address the capacity to learn abound, either by providing students with an opportunity to practice problem-solving skills or by providing constructive, timely feedback on their progress. All students benefit from engaging in the practices of the field such as research, and underrepresented students should be offered particular opportunities to do so. Flexible curriculum structures, such as booster modules for spatial visualization skills (see engaginginengineering.org), provide students with access to requisite skills and the means to merge onto a STEM pathway.[24]

Does this mean that all students can succeed in STEM? It is always possible some will not. If you are interested in improving the recruitment and persistence of students from diverse backgrounds, however, you must take a closer look at how your department demonstrates a commitment toward helping students increase their capacity in STEM in courses and in cocurricular experiences.

Capacity: Reader Questions

- What opportunities does your department offer to students to gain confidence or strengthen their capacity for STEM?
- Do students have access to quality and timely feedback in their courses?
- Do faculty believe that students can grow in their ability?
- Do you currently conduct pretests for spatial or quantitative skills?

- Do students who test poorly on pretests have access to remediation course work?
- Where do students learn about, practice, or grapple with the subject outside class?
- How do students gain confidence in their problem-solving or research skills?
- How are students from various demographic groups performing in their courses?
- How do students feel about their experiences in their courses?

Interest

When students are interested in STEM topics, they are more likely to persist.[25] Interest can be positively influenced by a perception of relevance or usefulness in the future.[26] Alternatively, the combination of enjoyment and challenge can foster interest.[27] STEM courses are notorious for covering a lot of material, sometimes in a surface-level, disconnected way that does not present opportunities for deeper engagement.[28] Many faculty insist that students need to cover the basics before tackling the interesting and challenging work of STEM. When only basics are covered, however, students often struggle to see the relevance of their learning, whether pertaining to the world at large, their own lives, or the lives of the people in their community.[29]

Information also shapes interest: It's difficult to be interested in something you don't know about. Many students lack information about STEM careers or do not understand or are unaware of the academic pathways or cocurricular activities that will assist them in reaching their goals. Having a parent in STEM is still one of the biggest predictors of students' eventual pursuit of a career in STEM.[30] But some students do not have extensive family or community networks that offer connections to college-educated STEM professionals.[31] Some fields are still emerging, which makes information about these careers less accessible to students and families alike.

Students' interests may be diminished or enhanced by their perception of how feasible their plans are. Students may lack a clear road map of how to get into a particular career.[32] For example, they may not understand the importance of taking math prerequisites early in high school.[33] Some students miss out on cocurricular activities because of financial barriers.[34] Transfer students may be at a disadvantage in regard to letters of recommendation because they do not have as much time to get to know faculty at the four-year institution before needing to ask for a letter.[35]

Mentoring initiatives can encourage and solidify interest by promoting engagement in the professional practices of STEM fields. Initiatives can be created to involve students in the practices of STEM through course work or projects that students perceive as relevant to the world and to their communities. Chances for students to try out and participate in research, internships, and other special opportunities need to be as wide ranging and accessible as the course work.

Does every single lesson in STEM need to be relevant to the world? Not necessarily, but saving challenges and excitement for later in the major means losing the interest of many students and the opportunity to ignite that interest in others. Active learning practices, whether they involve asking provocative questions, engaging in peer debate, or undertaking challenging projects and research, can make a difference in not only engagement but also student comprehension and mastery of the subject matter. It's important to explore different ways to help students see the relevance of STEM to the world and that STEM careers can be engaging.

Interest: Reader Questions

- Where, how, and when do students develop their interest in STEM? Where are the opportunities?
- Do students lose their interest in your major? If so, where, how, and when?
- What do your enrollment patterns tell you about student interest in courses?
- Do students see the relevance of their learning? Where and how does that happen?
- Do students have access to key experiences or support services?
- How feasible is the completion of your STEM major? What are the obstacles?
- Where do students gain information about STEM careers or pathways?

Belongingness

Belongingness refers to a sense of shared identity—in this case, when one feels included or part of the STEM community.[36] When students feel that their identities are valued, or they find connections to others who share similar interests, they are more likely to feel a sense of belongingness and want to solidify their commitments to the field. Specific examples might be when students are invited to participate in class discussions or in the lab, recognized for their progress, or validated by those already in the field.[37] Invitations that span academic and cocurricular activities are especially powerful.[38] Recognition does not necessarily mean extrinsic rewards; rather, recognition may involve a STEM faculty member, an industry professional, or a more seasoned student showing interest in a student's learning, thereby signaling that the student is part of the STEM community, which promotes belongingness.[39]

Belongingness is a critical factor for individuals who are underrepresented in STEM. The current demographics of the workforce, including the people teaching and learning in our academic spaces, can send a negative signal to underrepresented students about their belongingness.[40] For example, women still make up less than 15% of students majoring in the physical sciences, computer science, or engineering fields. Students of color from African American and Latino backgrounds, not to mention women and faculty of color, are even fewer in number.[41] First-generation college students or low-income students in STEM may not feel a sense of community as many strive to work full-time and keep up in the competitive STEM classroom.[42] Research suggests that people feel their group is more visible and supported when the group's membership reaches a critical mass, typically at about 30% of the larger group.[43] By virtue of being underrepresented, and not being part of a critical mass, many students decide they do not belong.[44] Some students may consequently shift from one STEM field to another or from a STEM field to a non-STEM field where they perceive a better fit for people like them.[45] Indeed, some students may feel actively unwelcomed by people, circumstances, or the accepted status quo currently in the field.[46] Transfer students may give up their STEM major because they cannot complete the requirements as a result of sequencing and availability of courses in the fall semesters, which sends a message that STEM majors are only intended for nontransfer students.[47] Beyond the demographics, many students hold negative stereotypes about people who work in STEM careers.[48] For example, many students perceive that STEM is for "nerdy" people who do not value social relationships.[49] These perceptions discourage those who do not identify with these problematic stereotypes from further pursuing a career in STEM.[50]

While the classroom has the potential for community building, it may not be perceived by some students as a safe and welcoming place.[51] Underrepresented students may perceive STEM courses as uninviting or unwelcoming when they observe or experience negative or disrespectful interactions in the classrooms. They may see these courses as a glimpse of what the workplace will be like and decide against a career in the field as a result.[52] When students visit workplaces, they may encounter negative or stereotypical images, such as isolated cubicles, posters from popular sci-fi franchises, hallways filled with pictures of mostly male role models, or brochures that advertise color-blind philosophies instead of diversity (see Chapter 5, p. 90), all of which may discourage continued participation in STEM.[53]

Mentoring initiatives can be designed to increase access to professionals or peers who are a step or two ahead who share students' demographic characteristics and provide positive (or at least more diverse or complex) images of people in the field. Peer connections formed through collaborative learning in small groups or teams, whether during the transition to college, in gateway courses, or in capstone courses, boost students' sense of belongingness. Students who are given opportunities to engage in leadership roles may be more apt to see themselves connected to the profession and developing their professional identities as scientists or engineers.

Why should belongingness matter? Shouldn't it be enough to like science or math? The research consistently shows that social identities need to be considered, and for students who are underrepresented, more needs to be done to invite students into the field. (These efforts could help White male students who like collaboration and prefer horror movies to science fiction.) Thinking about how we validate and recognize students who possess a broad array of identities can go a long way in changing who studies in our department and who chooses to work there. Investing in these initiatives can have the added benefit of allowing all learners to feel a greater sense of belongingness and ability to thrive.

Belongingness: Reader Questions

- How do students feel about their belongingness in STEM? How do you know?
- Do students feel invited to participate in STEM fields? If so, how?
- Can a wide array of students access your curriculum?
- Do your classrooms, hallways, and other common spaces reflect diverse role models?
- What are students' experiences in courses, clubs, and workplaces?

The Big Picture: The Learning Environment and Departmental Climate

The ecological model helps us examine capacity, interest, and belongingness, first cast as factors that contribute to creating obstacles and then translated into opportunities for mentoring initiatives. We can see how these factors manifest themselves in the individual, the learning environment, and the broader departmental climate. The big picture helps us see the whole ecosystem and how to effectively take action in a broad sense as well as for specific individuals.

Consider an example in engineering. Students often arrive in our introductory engineering classes lacking the requisite spatial-visualization skills or confidence in their ability to solve problems. Much like the birds from the example at the beginning of this chapter, we realize that providing resources that address only the immediate problem—in this case, lacking spatial visualization problem-solving skills—without also looking carefully at ways we can transform the learning environment is a limited and limiting strategy. Mentoring initiatives can target the learning environment by strengthening the quality and timeliness of feedback provided in classrooms, building booster courses to remedy observed gaps in students' knowledge or skills, and creating a departmental climate in which everyone recognizes that when given support, students can learn and thrive despite gaps in their prior academic preparation. Thus, the students are not the only ones who can change to improve persistence; indeed, when the learning environment and the departmental climate change, we can create ecosystems that attract students and facilitate their persistence.

How does departmental climate contribute to persistence? [54] While there are many different indicators of climate, I focus on three in this book: representation, reputation, and resources.

Representation refers to the composition of the department or how diverse the faculty, staff, and student body are. We already reviewed how students are influenced by the prevailing images of those in the field and how the department contributes to students' sense of belonging by who studies and works in the department.[55]

Reputation means the ethos of the department and how inclusive or collegial students perceive the department to be.[56] A department's reputation is often informed by the psychological temperature (i.e., degree of chilliness or warmth) and how students experience daily interactions with faculty and staff in the department, such as in teaching and advising. When students perceive that faculty and staff are approachable, and they can ask questions, they are more apt to increase their capacity to learn as well as experience an increase in their interest.[57]

Resources includes financial or human capital, or other investments, needed to make things happen. They are also very important in regard to departmental culture. When department administrators invest in supporting professional development for faculty and staff, the department positions itself to provide innovative, inclusive teaching. When departments fund memberships in national organizations committed to diversifying STEM fields, they can more readily access guidelines on best practices. Without intentional resource allocations as well as internal policies regarding those resources, students and faculty might perceive that the department is giving only minimal lip service to mentoring, diversity, and persistence. Stated positively, motivation can be bolstered when departments see the alignment between resources and commitments.

One's department exists not only in an institution but also in a particular region, field and discipline, and society. Indeed, because the department exists in society, the departmental climate can be difficult to shift. By focusing on the indicators of the climate, you may find change more tangible and achievable. When we work with students and change the learning environment, we can shift climate through the resulting change in the department's reputation. Similarly, we can shift climate through our conversations about our hiring practices and our allocation of resources, which can shape the nature of learning experiences for students.

Departmental Climate: Reader Questions

- In the last year, have you talked about your course evaluations with your colleagues?
- In regard to the department, have you discussed how the courses fit together in your major?
- Do you have a good sense of how the departmental climate is perceived by students and colleagues? Where did you get this sense? Is there a recent climate study to review?
- What is the energy level or emotional temperature at your events or in your classrooms or study spaces?
- At the department level, have you discussed how you allocate time and resources to invest in your own learning as colleagues?

Reader Next Steps: Choose a Focus

We can change the persistence of STEM students by targeting small groups of individuals, learning environments, departmental climates, or all of these. Now that we have mapped a hypothetical landscape together, you can do the same and take a closer look at your own department. I encourage you to choose a focus for your efforts. While I think the big picture is very important, it is equally important to make your efforts manageable; otherwise, the scope of the work can feel overwhelming. I hope the following steps help you get started.

1. Review existing, available data. The good news is you might not need to collect anything new. Indeed, be cautious about sending out a survey or pulling together a group of students for focus groups without first checking on what you already have. If you already have data as a department, college, or institution, then you might inadvertently harm future data collection efforts. Start with what you have, and think deliberately about whether you need additional information (see Table 1.1.).

TABLE 1.1
Possible Data Sources and Indicators

Data sources: Where to look	Indicators: What to track
Institutional research	Institutional or national surveys with current students and alumni
Admissions	Academic and career interests, primary high schools or community colleges, financial aid information
Committee on inclusion; diversity task force	Climate study or report that includes perceptions of inclusion in advising and teaching on campus
Departments	Focus groups with graduating seniors, capstone projects or other sample assignments, department budget allocations for academic support services or memberships for professional organizations (e.g., Society of Women Engineers)
Provost, dean; human resources	Course evaluations, faculty turnover, handbook of policies
Registrar	Enrollments, majors, grades
Alumni relations	Alumni, positions held, types of graduate schools attended, fellowships

2. Choose a particular group of students to serve as a lens for further inquiry. Are you interested in learning about persistence from a particular vantage point? From women, students of color, African American students, transfer students, or low-income students? While the answer might be all of them, think about which group of underrepresented students will serve as a lens for your work so you can

see experiences from that group's perspective while acknowledging that not all students within a particular demographic perceive the world in the same way. It is important to note that choosing a focus for further inquiry does not preclude including all students in your efforts. By reviewing your department's enrollment, persistence, and graduation data, you will likely illuminate a priority lens for further inquiry and intervention (see Figure 1.1).

Figure 1.1 Which Students Will Serve as Lenses?

Students of color

Women

First-generation college students

Community-college transfer students

Another group:

3. Choose a particular transition in college. All the college years are important, of course, but it can help to target one particular transition to improve your focus, especially when resources are limited. Perhaps you just revamped your introductory curriculum but have not reviewed capstone courses. Maybe a recent external review of your department suggested that belongingness is an issue for students of color, or maybe you have reports from alumni about their struggles with their job search (see Figure 1.2).

Figure 1.2 Choosing a Transition.

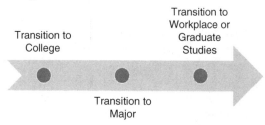

4. Consider which obstacles you will prioritize. Perhaps you want to build capacity to learn by investing in a spatial-visualization prerequisite, or maybe you want to look at reputation as a climate indicator (see Figure 1.3).

Figure 1.3 Your Primary Obstacle(s).

Capacity

Interest

Belongingness

Learning environment

Teaching or advising interactions

Representation

Reputation

Resources

Another obstacle:

5. See the mentoring opportunity within each obstacle. What might a mentoring initiative aim to achieve? (see Figure 1.4).

In the next chapter you will construct a mentoring strategy that aligns with the goals you identified here. You will conduct an inventory of what mentoring resources you already have before committing to new initiatives.

Figure 1.4 Your Primary Mentoring Goal(s).

Improve student competence or confidence in problem-solving skills

Create interest in STEM courses or department events

Connect students to each other or to professionals in field

Another goal:

Notes

1. Bronfenbrenner, U. (1979). *The ecology of human development.* Cambridge, MA: Harvard University Press.

2. Dowd, A. C. (2012). Developing supportive STEM community college to four-year college and university transfer ecosystems. In S. Olson & J. B. Labov (Eds.), *Community colleges in the evolving STEM education landscape: Summary of a summit* (pp. 35–40). Washington, DC: National Academies Press. Retrieved from download.nap.edu/catalog.php?record_id=13399

3. Mervis, J. (2010). Undergraduate science: Better intro courses seen as key to reducing attrition of STEM majors. *Science, 330*(6002), 306.

4. Eccles, J. S. (1994). Understanding women's educational and occupational choices. *Psychology of Women Quarterly, 18*(4), 585–609.

5. Stanger-Hall, K. (2012). Multiple-choice exams: An obstacle for higher-level thinking in introductory science classes. *CBE–Life Sciences Education, 11*(3), 294–306.

6. Wilson, Z., Holmes, L., deGravelles, K., Sylvain, M., Batiste, L., Johnson, M., . . . Warner, I. (2012). Hierarchical mentoring: A transformative strategy for improving diversity and retention in undergraduate STEM disciplines. *Journal of Science Education & Technology, 21*(1), 148–156. doi:10.1007/s10956-011-9292-5

7. Rattan, A., Good, C., & Dweck, C. S. (2012). "It's ok—not everyone can be good at math": Instructors with an entity theory comfort (and demotivate) students. *Journal of Experimental Social Psychology, 48*(3), 731–737.

8. Dweck, C. S., & Leggett, E. L. (1988). A social-cognitive approach to motivation and personality. *Psychological Review, 95*(2), 256–273.

9. Dweck, C. S. (2006). *Mindset: The new psychology of success.* New York, NY: Random House.

10. Rattan, A., Good, C., & Dweck, C. S. (2012). "It's ok—not everyone can be good at math": Instructors with an entity theory comfort (and demotivate) students. *Journal of Experimental Social Psychology, 48*(3), 731–737.

11. Hsi, S., Linn, M., & Bell, J. (1997). The role of spatial reasoning in engineering and the design of spatial instruction. *Journal of Engineering Education, 96*(2), 151–158.

12. Schunk, D. H. (1991). Self-efficacy and academic motivation. *Educational Psychologist, 26*(3/4), 207–231.

13. Lent, R. W., Brown, S. D., & Hackett, G. (1994). Toward a unifying social cognitive theory of career and academic interest, choice, and performance. *Journal of Vocational Behavior, 45*(1), 79–122.

14. Chi, M. T. H., Feltovich, P., & Glaser, R. (1981). Categorization and representation of physics problems by experts and novices. *Cognitive Science, 5*(2), 121–152.

15. Chang, M. J., Eagan, M. K., Lin, M. H., & Hurtado, S. (2011). Considering the impact of racial stigmas and science identity: Persistence among biomedical and behavioral science aspirants. *Journal of Higher Education, 82*(5), 564–596.

16. Mervis, J. (2010). Better intro courses seen as key to reducing attrition of STEM majors. *Science, 330*(6002), 306.

17. Schunk, D. H. (1991). Self-efficacy and academic motivation. *Educational Psychologist, 26*(3/4), 207–231.

18. Treisman, U. (1992). Studying students studying calculus: A look at the lives of minority mathematics students in college. *College Mathematics Journal, 23*(5), 362–372.

19. Chang, M. J., Eagan, M. K., Lin, M. H., & Hurtado, S. (2011). Considering the impact of racial stigmas and science identity: Persistence among biomedical and behavioral science aspirants. *Journal of Higher Education, 82*(5), 564–596.

20. Steele, C. M., & Aronson, J. (1997). A threat in the air: How stereotypes shape intellectual identity and performance. *American Psychologist, 52*(6), 613–629.

21. Aronson, J., Lustina, M. J., Good, C., Keough, K., Steele, C. M., & Brown, J. (1999). When White men can't do math: Necessary and sufficient factors in stereotype threat. *Journal of Experimental Social Psychology, 35*(1), 29–46.

22. Harackiewicz, J. M., Canning, E. A., Tibbetts, Y., Giffen, C. J., Blair, S. S., Rouse, D. I., & Hyde, J. S. (2014). Closing the social class achievement gap for first-generation college students in undergraduate biology. *Journal of Educational Psychology,* 106(2), 375–389.

23. Eddy, S. L., Brownell, S. E., & Wenderoth, M. P. (2014). Gender gaps in achievement and participation in multiple introductory biology classrooms. *CBE– Life Sciences Education, 13*(3), 478–492.

24. Martín-Dorta, N., Saorín, S. J., & Contero, M. (2008). Development of a fast remedial course to improve the spatial abilities of engineering students. *Journal of Engineering Education, 97*(4), 505–513.

25. Eccles, J. S. (1994). Understanding women's educational and occupational choices. *Psychology of Women Quarterly, 18*(4), 585–609.

26. Husman, J., & Lens, W. (1999). The role of the future in student motivation. *Educational Psychologist, 34*(2), 113–125.

27. Csikszentmihalyi, M. (2008). *Flow: The psychology of optimal experience.* New York, NY: Harper Perennial Modern Classics.

28. Crowe, A., Dirks, C., & Wenderoth, M. P. (2008). Biology in bloom: Implementing Bloom's taxonomy to enhance student learning in biology. *CBE–Life Sciences Education, 7*(4), 368–381.

29. Kilgore, D., Atman, C. J., Yasuhara, K., Barker, T. J., & Morozov, A. (2007). Considering context: A study of first-year engineering students. *Journal of Engineering Education, 96*(4), 321–334.

30. Harwell, E. (2012). *An analysis of parent occupation and student choice in STEM major.* Retrieved from stepup.education.illinois.edu/sites/default/files/EH%20 Parent%20Occ%20Brief.pdf

31. Hannover, B., & Kessels, U. (2004). Self-to-prototype matching as a strategy for making academic choices: Why high school students do not like math and science. *Learning and Instruction, 14*(1), 51–67.

32. Oyserman, D., Bybee, D., Terry, K., & Hart-Johnson, T. (2004). Possible selves as roadmaps. *Journal of Research in Personality, 38*(2), 130–149.

33. Packard, B. W., Babineau, M. E., & Machado, H. M. (2012). Becoming job-ready: Collaborative future plans of Latina adolescent girls and their mothers in a low-income urban community. *Journal of Adolescent Research*, 27(1), 110–131.

34. Bastedo, M. N., & Jaquette, O. (2011). Running in place: Low-income students and the dynamics of higher education stratification. *Educational Evaluation and Policy Analysis, 33*(3), 318–339.

35. Packard, B. W., Gagnon, J. L., LaBelle, O., Jeffers, K., & Lynn, E. (2011). Women's experiences in the STEM community college transfer pathway. *Journal of Women and Minorities in Science and Engineering, 17*(2), 129–147.

36. Good, C., Rattan, A., & Dweck, C. S. (2012). Why do women opt out? Sense of belonging and women's representation in mathematics. *Journal of Personality and Social Psychology, 102*(4), 700–717. doi:10.1037/a0026659

37. Carlone, H. B., & Johnson, A. (2007). Understanding the science experiences of successful women of color: Science identity as an analytic lens. *Journal of Research in Science Teaching, 44*(8), 1197–1218.

38. Hausmann, L., Schofield, J., & Woods, R. (2007). Sense of belonging as a predictor of intentions to persist among African American and White first-year college students. *Research in Higher Education, 48*(7), 803–839. doi:10.1007/s11162-007-9052-9

39. Carlone, H. B., & Johnson, A. (2007). Understanding the science experiences of successful women of color: Science identity as an analytic lens. *Journal of Research in Science Teaching, 44*(8), 1197–1218.

40. Johnson, D. R. (2012). Campus racial climate perceptions and overall sense of belonging among racially diverse women in STEM majors. *Journal of College Student Development, 53*(2), 336–346.

41. National Science Foundation. (2007). *Women, minorities, and persons with disabilities in science and engineering.* Arlington, VA: National Science Foundation. Retrieved from ERIC database. (ED496396)

42. Wilson, R. E., & Wilson, J. (2013). Science as a classed and gendered endeavor: Persistence of two White female first-generation college students within an undergraduate science context. *Journal of Research in Science Teaching, 50*(7), 802–825.

43. Hagedorn, L. S., Chi, W. Y., Cepeda, R. M., & McLain, M. (2007). An investigation of critical mass: The role of Latino representation in the success of urban community college students. *Research in Higher Education, 48*(1), 73–91.

44. Good, C., Rattan, A., & Dweck, C. S. (2012). Why do women opt out? Sense of belonging and women's representation in mathematics. *Journal of Personality and Social Psychology, 102,* 700–717. doi:10.1037/a0026659

45. Packard, B. W., & Nguyen, D. (2003). Science career-related possible selves of adolescent girls: A longitudinal study. *Journal of Career Development, 29*(4), 251–263.

46. Jackson, S. M., Hillard, A. L., & Schneider, T. R. (2014). Using implicit bias training to improve attitudes toward women in STEM. *Social Psychology of Education, 17*(3), 419–438.

47. Packard, B. W., Gagnon, J. L., LaBelle, O., Jeffers, K., & Lynn, E. (2011). Women's experiences in the STEM community college transfer pathway. *Journal of Women and Minorities in Science and Engineering, 17*(2), 129–147.

48. Cundiff, J. L., Vescio, T. K., Loken, E., & Lo, L. (2013). Do gender–science stereotypes predict science identification and science career aspirations among undergraduate science majors? *Social Psychology of Education, 16*(4), 541–554. doi:10.1007/s11218-013-9232-8

49. Diekman, A. B., Brown, E. R., Johnston, A. M., & Clark, E. K. (2010). Seeking congruity between roles and goals: A new look at why women opt out of STEM careers. *Psychological Science, 21*(8), 1051–1057.

50. Jones, B., Ruff, C., & Paretti, M. (2013). The impact of engineering identification and stereotypes on undergraduate women's achievement and persistence in engineering. *Social Psychology of Education, 16*(3), 471–493. doi:10.1007/s11218-013-9222-x

51. Tinto, V. (1997). Classrooms as communities: Exploring the educational character of student persistence. *Journal of Higher Education, 68*(6), 599–623.

52. Amelink, C. T., & Creamer, E. G. (2010). Gender differences in elements of the undergraduate experience that influence satisfaction with the engineering major and the intent to pursue engineering as a career. *Journal of Engineering Education, 99*(1), 81–92.

53. Plaut, V. C., Thomas, K. M., & Goren, M. J. (2009). Is multiculturalism or color blindness better for minorities? *Psychological Science, 20*(4), 444–446.

54. Johnson, D. R. (2012). Campus racial climate perceptions and overall sense of belonging among racially diverse women in STEM majors. *Journal of College Student Development, 53*(2), 336–346.

55. Locks, A. M., Hurtado, S., Bowman, N. A., & Oseguera, L. (2008). Extending notions of campus climate and diversity to students' transition to college. *Review of Higher Education, 31*(3), 257–285.

56. Porath, C. L., & Pearson, C. M. (2010). The cost of bad behavior. *Organizational Dynamics, 39*(1), 64–71.

57. Gasiewski, J. A., Eagan, K., Garcia, G., Hurtado, S., & Chang, M. J. (2012). From gatekeeping to engagement: A multicontextual, mixed method study of student engagement in introductory STEM courses. *Research in Higher Education, 53*(2), 229–261. doi:10.1007/s11162-011-9247-y

2

MENTORING WITH INTENTION

What's Your Strategy?

I n this chapter, I guide you through developing a mentoring strategy by examining an array of approaches that can help you achieve your goals. I encourage you to start small and to take an inventory of your existing resources before committing to new initiatives. At the end of this chapter, you will construct a road map to see if your plans make sense.

Intentional Mentoring

In this book, I define *mentoring* as a developmental experience intended to help students develop, increase their capacity to learn, and encourage persistence in the field.[1] We (faculty and staff) create mentoring initiatives to support more students rather than leave mentoring to chance.[2] An intentional approach to mentoring means you start with the outcomes you want for students and consider how mentors can help students achieve them (see Figure 2.1). All too often, designers start to organize a mentoring program without first identifying the goals for the initiative and detailing how the planned mentoring will address what they need. Anyone familiar with using backward design in teaching will be familiar with the approach of starting with your learning outcomes before designing your instruction.[3] The same process is applicable to mentoring design. After reading this chapter, I hope you will be more likely to invest in the kind of mentoring that will help you reach your outcomes.

Knowing what you want to achieve will help you think about the design and intention of your initiative. We often do have specific outcomes in mind, such as increasing student competence in problem solving in math or science, helping students advance to an upper-level course, or encouraging a stronger sense of belongingness in the classroom. In Chapter 1, I suggest

Figure 2.1 Intentional approach to mentoring.

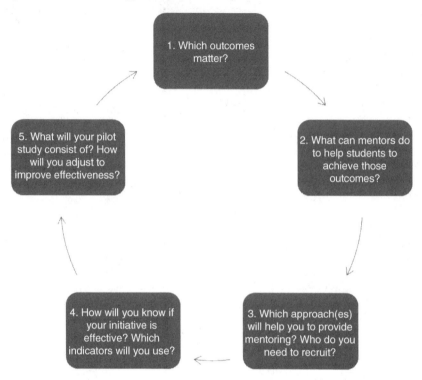

that you reflect on the outcomes most relevant to you and your department. Typical student outcomes include

- increased confidence in one's abilities (self-efficacy);
- greater knowledge or competence, such as in problem solving,
- stronger interest, demonstrated by the courses students take or their intention to pursue a career;
- greater sense of belonging or connection to the field; and
- persistence or advancement in one's path, such as declaring a major, completing a major, or securing a position in the field after graduation.

Knowing which outcomes you want to achieve will help you decide which mentors you ask to participate and how they can help students in your initiative. For example, mentors can be asked to encourage students to persist by acting as role models, assuring students that they belong in the field, advising students on the pathway toward careers, providing feedback on or strategies for completing academic work, coaching their research process, or acting as a sponsor by recommending students for opportunities. The initiative focuses mentors' actions in ways that make sense; for example, your initiative will ask mentors to validate students' sense of belongingness if that is one of your key outcomes. Thus, advising or providing feedback on academic work, while valuable, may not be relevant for every single initiative you design, as illustrated in this example.

Ultimately, knowing what you need mentors to do will help you decide which approaches to use and whom to recruit as a mentor. Before delving into these details and ways to track your progress, I want to explain how building a network is a critical part of an effective mentoring strategy. Research supports a network-based approach to mentoring with a constellation of mentors; that is, an effective mentoring initiative typically draws in people with different skill sets and resources in different stages of their careers (ranging from peer mentors through seasoned professional mentors) and different domains (including college-based mentors and workplace mentors).[4] A diverse network of mentors is more likely to produce more and better quality mentoring than relying on just one mentor to do it all.[5] In STEM fields, networks of cross-level clusters, sometimes termed *cascade* mentoring or *hierarchical* mentoring, are very common. In this model, faculty, graduate students, seasoned students, and newer students all contribute.[6]

For example, in supplemental instruction programs, students may be grouped into peer learning teams to practice problem solving, with the new students guided by seasoned peers who serve as supplemental instructors and are supervised by a graduate student or a faculty director with ongoing support from the professor teaching the course. In a research team, we often observe similar clustering of individuals across levels.[7] Other mentor clusters are deliberately constructed across domains of work in which faculty at the college or university facilitate student access to industry professionals.[8] Each part of the network lends itself to providing particular kinds of support. For example, peer mentors are especially capable of providing encouragement and a sense of belongingness through cohort-building activities, while industry professionals are especially adept at providing connections to the field.[9] Be cognizant of the particular composition of such a network to capitalize on the strengths of particular mentors in ways that align with your goals.

Approaches to Mentoring

Many approaches can be used to provide mentoring; we need different approaches to achieve different outcomes.[10] Of course, the array of approaches can also make it challenging to decide what to choose. To assist you in your decision making, I include here a discussion of some approaches with their pros and cons: events, programs, practices, and policies. These approaches are complementary and collectively contribute to a comprehensive strategy.

Events

Events are typically one-time, intensive conferences or seminars that are designed for a specific purpose. For example, they could introduce students to networking opportunities with prospective mentors or increase students' knowledge of a career in the field. Events can involve career panels (featuring speakers), employer site visits, shared meals, or speed networking. The mentoring can take place remotely using Skype or social media. Mentoring could even take place at a less conventional event such as a computer science 24-hour hackathon. Mentoring can include providing the financial means or taking care of the logistics for students to attend the annual meeting of a national organization or by creating a local chapter of a national organization that can host events.[11]

Often, a mentoring program begins as an event or a set of events; you can develop a program slowly by piloting a set of events and gauging their impact. An event can be a strategic way to start small in order to build a program. Alternatively, an event may be envisioned from the beginning as a stand-alone one-time event to positively improve the department climate by way of its reputation as a place for exciting events. The main downside of an event-based model is that one-time events may not produce a lasting impact linked to persistence. However, in the case of information sharing or inspiration, one-time events can be effective and contribute at least in part to efforts to encourage students to persist.

Event-Based Initiatives: Reader Questions

- Do you want to influence many students or a select few? Events are helpful for affecting larger groups of students and often require fewer resources because they happen only once or twice.
- Is your goal very particular and achievable with a short duration of contact? For example, are you aiming to spark students' enthusiasm to learn more or to disseminate key information? One intensive event can be effective if designed well. Think carefully about the energy of that one event and the message the event is sending.

Programs

Programs are designed to provide mentoring directly to a set of participants through an organized schedule of ongoing meetings or events. The designer constructs the mentoring program, students are invited or recruited to enroll, and mentors are recruited to serve for a certain amount of time with particular goals in mind. Programs typically have a beginning (orientation, training, or kick-off event), middle (ongoing meetings), and end (concluding ceremony or announcement of the program's end). Most mentoring programs are face-to-face, although they can take place remotely, if necessary.[12] In addition, in many programs students are matched with mentors one-on-one, although group mentoring programs involving teams of mentors and students or shorter mentoring rotations involving multiple mentors sequentially are also effective approaches.[13] A particularly common model is cascade mentoring in which newer students engage in research with the support of seasoned peers, a faculty member, and often a postdoc or lab manager.[14]

Programs target small numbers of individuals when designers want the program to be selective. Many programs aim for a particular group of underrepresented students (e.g., women, students of color, community college transfer students), but it depends on what the funding agency permits or what the institution can support.[15] In many situations, criteria must be broadened to provide access to a wider group of applicants in ways that permit affinity clusters of underrepresented students and participation from students at large.

Although mentoring programs can produce incredible results, they tend to be expensive because they are so intensive; therefore, they can only serve a limited number of students.[16] The intensity of a program can also discourage participation. Further, using a one-on-one model can sometimes end

---

Program-Based Initiatives: Reader Questions

- Do you want to influence many students or a select few? Programs are helpful for targeting a select group of students.
- Do you have many outcomes in mind for these students? Programs are often used when you have multiple goals in mind.
- Do you have access to necessary resources, including time, a pool of mentors, and finances? Programs tend to be expensive depending on the experiences provided and the intensity of the time commitment. Be judicious in selecting whom you ask to play a role and how the person plays it.

in disappointment when the mentor fails to provide everything the student desires.[17] Although students in mentoring programs may have good experiences, unless those experiences are reinforced more broadly in the learning environment and in the department, the positive effects from the program will likely be lessened. Without training for mentors and students, the potential effectiveness is diminished.[18]

Practices

Practices are initiatives that embed mentoring into teaching and advising to improve or maximize the informal mentoring that already occurs in those settings. Informal interactions with key individuals such as advisers or instructors are repeatedly cited as influencing student motivation or facilitating student success through providing information or other kinds of support.[19] Because this approach to mentoring targets core practices within the learning environment, educators can be more inclusive, reaching many students at a time. For the most part, mentoring practices integrated into classes or advising interactions can be implemented at a lower cost or with minimal additional effort. That being said, practices of the department are influenced by the availability of resources. For example, resources will determine whether academic peer mentors are integrated into one course or five courses, or whether faculty have the time and support to attend a seminar focused on inclusive teaching pedagogies.

When mentoring is integrated into the learning environment, students will not necessarily perceive that they are being provided with a special intervention. Depending on the nature of the initiative, students may or may not perceive the initiative as impactful. A challenge is to involve the entire department or the curriculum as a whole; it is more common for one instructor or one course at a time to be transformed.[20]

Practice-Based Initiatives: Reader Questions

- Do you want to influence many students or a select few? Practice-based initiatives are helpful for reaching many students.
- Do particular practices such as advising or teaching provide a vehicle for facilitating the kind of mentoring you envision? Implementing a practice is feasible when you can influence key courses or advising practices.
- Do you have access to these instructors or advisers? Are they interested in participating? The success of practice-based initiatives relies on these considerations.

Policies

Department administrators may choose to develop or change a policy to increase student access to mentoring events, programs, and practices. They may notice the small, individual decisions on the investments being made in mentoring activities and see the need for a general policy decision about how resources are allocated. Policies can also help departments move from individual-level, haphazard decision making to coordinated, planned, collaborative decision making. Policy decisions often beneficially influence climate by enhancing the reputation of the department.

For example, a department may require a commitment to a specific mentoring outcome for anyone seeking internal funding to support a summer student, such as an explicit plan for how the undergraduate student will gain career-relevant skills. Or, to reinforce to their commitment to inclusivity, department administrators may decide to implement a policy of providing at least one copy, depending on class size, of each required book to be placed on reserve in the library for any student in the class to check out.

Administrators can ask themselves whether and how their resource allocations align with their commitments. Specifically, the department budget can be reviewed to see if particular events, programs, or practices have enough financial support. Then administrators can review existing policies and determine whether certain policies could help them state their priorities clearly.

Policy-Based Initiatives: Reader Questions

- Do your policies and associated resource allocations reflect your commitments? Taking a close look at how you provide books on reserve, rotate core courses, and allocate academic support services can be a good starting point for policy.
- How does the department decide which initiatives receive funding and which ones do not? You might decide to modify an existing policy following a collective discussion.

Making Decisions: Intensity and Selectivity

To review the factors that will contribute to your decision making, return to your desired goals or outcomes and consider how intense your initiative needs to be and which students and mentors should be selected to participate. These considerations should be raised at the outset and revisited as you continue to read about, design, and reconsider your plans in subsequent chapters.

To achieve a particular goal, say, a strong attachment between a traditional-age student and an adult, students and mentors might need regular contact over a yearlong period; typically, a close personal connection is not created by meeting someone once or twice. Many of us are familiar with the Big Brothers Big Sisters program in which an adult mentor is matched with a young person, usually from a single-parent household, for an intensive year to foster a positive attachment to the adult mentor (see www.bbbs.org). Research demonstrates that mentoring is associated with better academic and personal outcomes such as friendships and positive adult relationships for young people, as long as the adult mentors are reliable and uphold their yearlong commitment.[21]

When considering STEM persistence in college, the need for such intensity is rare. The closest approximation is a summer research program that lasts at least eight weeks. The duration of these programs is often driven by what is considered to be the minimum number of weeks needed for students to achieve mastery of a specific research process. A similar impact can be achieved without full immersion through a research course that meets for fewer hours spread out over a longer period (e.g., a 14-week semester).[22] To provide more accurate career information, a designer might envision one or two highly informative advising sessions over coffee or after class, which demonstrates that a less intensive commitment can nevertheless have a positive impact.

Many of you who are considering a program-based approach to mentoring may wrestle with the tension between inclusivity and selectivity. How do you justify investing so much in a few students? If you scale back the intensity, however, will the initiative be effective for *any* students? This is not an easy decision, but your particular primary goals and institutional, departmental, or demographic context may help you. For example, if you are in a department with very few women students, deciding to invest in a program selectively designed for them may make sense. If your primary issue stems from a core gateway course, then investing in that course to benefit all those enrolled is a strategic plan. If you would like to invest in enrolling students in the gateway courses and in the capstone courses but can't do both, you will have to determine whether your priorities should focus more on recruiting students into the major or helping declared majors enter the workforce. The key is being intentional about what you are hoping to achieve and being committed to tracking your progress. Even if you have a particular target group of students in mind (e.g., women or African American students), you can choose to create an initiative that invests in their persistence and benefits students in your department as well. For example, you might deliberately recruit an affinity group of African American students to participate in a program that is open to all students and track the progress of African Americans as well as the participants as a whole.

Selecting mentors can also be a challenge. You want mentors who are adept at providing what you need. While demographically similar mentors can be powerful for underrepresented students, such mentors are in short supply.[23] Where possible, take advantage of peer mentors, partnerships among peer institutions, alumni networks, or professional associations to increase your access to mentors from underrepresented backgrounds. In addition, draw from a heterogeneous set of mentors across gender and race, creating a type of network associated with positive outcomes.[24] Moreover, when you enlist a wider array of mentors, you can share the mentoring responsibility while exposing students to a wider array of perspectives.[25] Providing training and support for students and mentors will help, whether you are enlisting demographically similar or demographically different mentors.

Think carefully about the role of the peer mentors, capitalizing on what they can do but keeping in mind that they need some support from supervisors. At the same time be judicious in your requests of professional-level mentors, including faculty.[26] This is one reason a cascade model is so popular: The power of peers is put to use while relying respectfully (and wisely) on the professional-level mentors as supervisors and guides.

Start Small With a Pilot

Even if you have unlimited resources and can ramp up a program to a large scale right away, I still recommend that you find a way to start small. Starting small might mean trying out an event instead of launching a full-fledged program, or it might mean working with one class or a small group of advisers instead of bringing all courses and all advisers into alignment at the outset. We often refer to starting small using the term *pilot testing*.[27]

Following pilot testing, you can adjust your approach. For example, let's say you included a career panel as a component of a longer mentoring program, and you find out that the panel actually discouraged the students. Maybe you designed a summer research initiative from which participants really benefited, but students were confused by the role of the peer mentors. Maybe many students and faculty emerged with a set of unresolved questions after a training module. Through pilot testing, you often learn what needs to be intensified, what needs to be removed or added, and what needs to be modified.

If you are applying for a grant, your pilot work will provide you with some evidence that you are on the right track or how you can get there. Funders will often want to see proof of concept or that what you are proposing has the capacity to work. Many stakeholders want a chance to see a program in action before committing further resources or increasing the scope of its reach. Complaints that key people were not consulted are far less likely if you implement a pilot program first. In reality, all initiatives involve an iterative process of revision, but the word *pilot* communicates more clearly that revision is likely.

Reader Next Steps: Create a Road Map

One of the most important considerations at this stage is to take stock of what you already have in place and what will be feasible to achieve with those resources. Many good ideas are generated but lack the proper infrastructure or mechanism to be properly implemented. In the following section I describe an array of evidence-based approaches used at several different campuses and evidence-based explanations for why they work. Chapters 3, 4, and 5 focus on the three key transitions of the college experience, allowing you to decide which of the ideas presented might be worth trying in your department and context, using the case study provided as a catalyst for brainstorming. Choosing something new might mean adapting an existing structure or reallocating resources so you can invest in a replacement intervention. I remind you to start small and pilot test your initiatives. Now, consider the following set of next steps.

What does your road map look like? You will find it helpful to map your plan to see where you are going. Take a minute to reflect on your desired outcomes and what you will need to achieve them. In program design, this mapping is often referred to as a *logic model* because the designer maps the logical relationships among investments, activities, and the intended outcomes to see if they make sense.[28] (To learn more, visit the University of Wisconsin-Extension website, www.uwex.edu/ces/pdande/evaluation/evallogicmodel.html). The series of prompts in Figure 2.2 is an example of a road map.

Figure 2.2 Road map.

My desired outcome is_____

The rationale is_____

I am going to try this approach (event/program/practice/policy)_____

I will need these resources_____

I already have these resources_____

I will know if the program is successful because_____

My pilot study will include_____

Figure 2.3 Logic model.

I will invest_____
to create_____.
If I do_____, then I expect
_____.
If that happens, then_____.

Writing a series of if/then statements to outline the logic of your model will also help. A general format might be, "If I invest [X] in order to do [Y], then I can expect [Z]," as illustrated by the following:

If I invest money [X] to hire mentors to provide college students with information about the academic pathway [Y], *then* the students will increase their knowledge of which courses to take and feel more connected to someone in the field [Z]. *If* I do that, *then* the college students will be more apt to report confidence in their knowledge and take the right courses. *If* that happens, *then* our department will report a larger number of enrollments and majors.

The idea is to map out your logic to see if what you plan makes sense in terms of linking it to your expected outcomes. Remember to start with the outcome you want, and think about the programs, practices, events, or policies that might help you reach that outcome. See Figure 2.3 for more general constructions of logic models.

What resources will you have access to? You should spend some time taking stock of your resources. Be candid about what you will need to achieve your desired outcome. Then you can determine if you have the necessary resources to carry out that plan. If not, you might try to scale back your plan or try alternative approaches that are less expensive or less intensive.

What programming do you already have? Do you have any programming that can be adapted or repurposed? Rather than create something new, is it possible for you to collaborate with an existing program or end a program that does not appear to be working well and then try something new? Do you have a tutoring program that is not producing the outcomes you hope for? Maybe you can repurpose this programming in favor of something more effective. Or perhaps you have an excellent orientation program you could add a breakout session to for STEM transfer students.

Will you have access to sufficient funds? Find out what money in your budget is allocated for initiatives of the type you envision and if there are funds you could apply for elsewhere in the college or university. If you are intending to apply for an external grant, consider what you can launch without the additional funds and what the additional funding will permit you to do. What you can do right now could serve as your pilot test, and the pilot could be used to justify further investment.

Is this plan sustainable? If you require external funding for the project, you should also ask how you plan to sustain the project after the grant is over.

Who will you involve? Do you have a ready pool of mentors across career stages or domains of higher education and industry? Will they need training? How will you balance mentors across gender and race? Do you have access to the instructors of core courses or to advisers? Do you have any collaborators, such as someone in a social science or education field or someone working in another relevant office on campus? Most grants require an external evaluator. Do you have someone in mind?

How will you know if your initiative has had an impact? Refer to the data sources you consulted in Chapter 1 to identify ways to measure the impact. Will you be looking for increased enrollments or more positive student feedback on academic support in a core course? Think about how you will measure the impact of any pilot you launch. Visit assessmentcommons.org or the assessment section of the American Association of Colleges & Universities website (www.aacu.org/resources/assessment) for tools that can help you. If you are working with a particular funder, consider the kinds of outcomes necessary to establish progress or to illustrate impact from the funder's viewpoint. The external evaluator or a colleague with experience in educational and social science research or in assessment can help you analyze your overall plan and each component of your initiative.

Refine your plans by exploring ideas on other campuses. To help you refine your plans, the next three chapters discuss promising research-based approaches used on several campuses. You can focus on a specific chapter (Chapter 3, transition to college; Chapter 4, transition to STEM major; Chapter 5, transition to workplace or graduate studies), or you might also decide to skim through recent issues of various publications. Most disciplines have an educational or applied journal (e.g., *Journal of Engineering Education*, *Journal of Chemical Education*) that can provide good ideas to inform your plans.

Notes

1. Kram, K. (1985). *Mentoring at work: Developmental relationships in organizational life*. Glenview, IL: Scott Foresman.

2. Blake-Beard, S. D. (2001). Taking a hard look at formal mentoring programs: A consideration of potential challenges facing women. *Journal of Management Development, 20*(4), 331–345; Chun, J. U., Sosik, J. J., & Yun, N. Y. (2012).

A longitudinal study of mentor and protégé outcomes in formal mentoring relationships. *Journal of Organizational Behavior, 33*(8), 1071–1094.

3. Wiggins, G., & McTighe, J. (2006). *Understanding by design.* Pearson Merrill Prentice Hall: Upper Saddle River, NJ.

4. Higgins, M. C., & Thomas, D. A. (2001). Constellations and careers: Toward understanding the effects of multiple developmental relationships. *Journal of Organizational Behavior, 22*(3), 223–247.

5. Packard, B. W., Kim, G. J., Sicley, M., & Piontkowski, S. (2009). Composition matters: Multi-context informal mentoring networks for low-income urban adolescent girls pursuing healthcare careers. *Mentoring & Tutoring: Partnerships in Learning, 17*(2), 187–200.

6. Wilson, Z., Holmes, L., deGravelles, K., Sylvain, M., Batiste, L., Johnson, M., . . . Warner, I. (2012). Hierarchical mentoring: A transformative strategy for improving diversity and retention in undergraduate STEM disciplines. *Journal of Science Education & Technology, 21*(1), 148–156.

7. Packard, B. W., Marciano, V., Payne, J. M., Bledzki, L. A., & Woodard, C. T. (2014). Negotiating peer mentoring roles in undergraduate research lab settings. *Mentoring & Tutoring: Partnerships in Learning, 22*(5), 433–445.

8. Chemers, M. M., Zurbriggen, E. L., Syed, M., Goza, B. K., & Bearman, S. (2011). The role of efficacy and identity in science career commitment among underrepresented minority students. *Journal of Social Issues, 67*(3), 469–491. doi:10.1111/j.1540-4560.2011.01710.x

9. Ensher, E. A., Thomas, C., & Murphy, S. E. (2001). Comparison of traditional, step-ahead, and peer mentoring on protégés' support, satisfaction, and perceptions of career success: A social exchange perspective. *Journal of Business and Psychology, 15*, 419–438.

10. Packard, B. W. (2003). Web-based mentoring: Challenging traditional models to increase women's access. *Mentoring & Tutoring, 11*(1), 53–65.

11. Gibson, C., Hardy, J. H., & Buckley, M. R. (2014). Understanding the role of networking in organizations. *The Career Development International, 19*(2), 146–161.

12. Crisp, G., & Cruz, I. (2009). Mentoring college students: A critical review of the literature between 1990 and 2007. *Research in Higher Education, 50*(6), 525–545.

13. Hall, D. M., Curtin-Soydan, A., & Canelas, D. A. (2014). The science advancement through group engagement program: Leveling the playing field and increasing retention in science. *Journal of Chemical Education, 91*(1), 37–47.

14. Edgcomb, M. R., Crowe, H. A., Rice, J. D., Morris, S. J., Wolffe, R. J., & McConnaughay, K. D. (2010). Peer and near-peer mentoring: Enhancing learning in summer research programs. *Council on Undergraduate Research Quarterly, 31*(2), 18–25.

15. Most programs targeting students of color have expanded to include low-income students or first-generation college students from any racial background. For more on the legal impact of offering programs based on race or gender, see www.aaup.org/what-now-michigan-cases-2004

16. Harper, S. R., & Griffin, K. A. (2010–2011). Opportunity beyond affirmative action: How low-income and working-class Black male achievers access highly selective, high-cost colleges and universities. *Harvard Journal of African American Public Policy, 17,* 43–60; Barlow, A. E. L., & Villarejo, M. (2004). Making a difference for minorities: Evaluation of an educational enrichment program. *Journal of Research in Science Teaching, 41*(9), 861–881.

17. Packard, B. W. (2003). Student training promotes mentoring awareness and action. *Career Development Quarterly, 51*(4), 335–345.

18. Kasprisin, C. A., Single, P. B., Single, R. M., Ferrier, J. L., & Muller, C. B. (2008). Improved mentor satisfaction: Emphasising protégé training for adult age mentoring dyads. *Mentoring & Tutoring: Partnership in Learning, 16*(2), 163–174.

19. Baker, V. L., & Griffin, K. A. (2010). Beyond mentoring and advising: Toward understanding the role of faculty "developers" in student success. *About Campus, 14*(6), 2–8.

20. Breslow, L. (2010). Wrestling with pedagogical change: The TEAL initiative at MIT. *Change, 42*(5), 23–29.

21. Grossman, J. B., & Rhodes, J. E. (2002). The test of time: Predictors and effects of duration in youth mentoring relationships. *American Journal of Community Psychology, 30*(2), 199–219.

22. Gibson, B. A., & Bruno, B. C. (2012). The C-MORE scholars program: Motivations for an academic-year research experiences for undergraduates program. *Journal of College Science Teaching, 43*(5), 12–18.

23. Blake-Beard, S., Bayne, M. L., Crosby, F. J., & Muller, C. B. (2011). Matching by race and gender in mentoring relationships: Keeping our eyes on the prize. *Journal of Social Issues, 67*(3), 622–643.

24. Thomas, D. A., & Gabarro, J. J. (1999). *Breaking through: The making of minority executives in corporate America.* Cambridge, MA: Harvard Business Review Press.

25. Packard, B. W. (2003). Web-based mentoring: Challenging traditional models to increase women's access. *Mentoring & Tutoring, 11*(1), 53–65.

26. Schwartz, J. (2012). Faculty as undergraduate research mentors for students of color: Taking into account the costs. *Science Education, 96,* 527–542.

27. Sproull, N. L. (2003). *Handbook of research methods: A guide for practitioners and students in the social sciences* (2nd ed.). Lanham, MD: Scarecrow Press.

28. Zimmerman, L., Kamal, Z., & Kim, H. (2013). Pedagogy of the logic model: Teaching undergraduates to work together to change their communities. *Journal of Prevention & Intervention in the Community, 41*(2), 121–127.

3

WHAT WORKS (AND WHY) DURING THE TRANSITION TO COLLEGE

D uring the transition to college, capacity, interest, and belongingness are critical factors in STEM recruitment and persistence. Department administrators have a tremendous opportunity to establish a reputation for innovation and inclusion, which can fuel students' initial interest and motivate them to take a second look at your field. This is the transition where the number of college students already open to or interested in STEM will be the largest. What department administrators and faculty do to validate and further cultivate student interest will critically impact persistence.

In this chapter, I place belongingness and interest at the forefront. Upon their arrival at a college or university, students, especially underrepresented students, are considering how they fit in with the institution in general and with STEM specifically.[1] Students closely examine academic fit (i.e., whether they are enthusiastic about their courses, which majors are offered at the institution), and social fit (i.e., availability of a peer group in the classroom or in cocurricular activities). For many students, interest in STEM is influenced by the activities they choose *and* the people they participate with in these activities, while introductory course work and department events provide students with a preview of the STEM major. Belongingness and interest are also influenced by the department's reputation, the person or people who are teaching or hosting events, and resources.

Emphasizing the capacity to learn also matters. For the many students who may have decided they are not capable, the challenge to persist is a bit different. Involving these students in STEM activities, whether in course work or a cocurricular event, in which they experience initial success is a powerful way to encourage students to take another look at STEM. Keep in mind that not all students have been exposed to the full range of STEM disciplines in high school or even in community college, and therefore they may not yet have an accurate idea of their capacity to learn or even a clear sense of their interests. For example, a student may say, "I am not a math person" but go on to excel in statistics, computer science, or biology, much to his or her surprise. New students need to have places where they can get involved with various fields of study and discover possibilities.

The Transition to College: Questions Students Ask

- Do I fit in at this institution?
- Are the STEM courses and cocurricular activities interesting to me?
- Does this department host events that I want and am able to attend?
- Do I believe that I can be successful in STEM?
- Are there peers I can engage with in STEM courses and activities?
- Are people who are like me valued here? Specifically, are people like me valued in STEM spaces?

What Works and Why

In this section, I spotlight STEM scholar mentoring programs as a promising approach to address all three major factors of student recruitment and persistence in STEM (capacity, interest, belongingness) during the transition to college. After participating in STEM scholar mentoring programs, students generally emerge with greater interest, a stronger sense of their capacity to learn, and a deeper connection or sense of belongingness in STEM. The approaches vary in terms of resources and intensity. Consider which might work well for your department and institution.

Spotlight: STEM Scholar Mentoring Programs

A promising approach to mentoring new college students is a STEM scholar mentoring program, which improves students' sense of belonging by creating an initial peer group of students with similar academic interests, among other positive outcomes. Scholar programs reinforce the feeling of power that comes with being part of a team; they cultivate a sense of belongingness, which in turn can buffer students in times of struggle and bolster their motivation to persist.[2] Scholar programs also typically include participation in STEM activities such as research or field trips and provide STEM-specific advising. The peer cohort enrolled in the program provides exposure to multiple positive and diverse role models beyond the involvement of any other mentors.

Scholar programs are especially effective in bolstering the persistence of first-generation college students, low-income students, and students of color.[3] Given the robust research documenting these programs' positive outcomes for students, whether that outcome is completion of a STEM major or the pursuit of graduate studies, STEM scholar programs have become a staple at many institutions that have the ability to finance the program, whether through an active federal grant, a private foundation, an endowed fund, or an admissions recruiting fund.

Scholar programs work well when the following four conditions are met.

1. *Scholar programs are small in terms of cohort size.* Much like the research on class size, research on mentoring suggests that smaller groups, such as the size of Posse Scholars (described in detail in the next section), are more effective than larger ones.[4] When students are part of a small team, it can help them feel more integrated and connected to the student body.[5]

2. *Scholar programs are highly selective.* Students are invited to enter the program and are selected based on their affinity for the group's purpose. In other words, they have a shared commitment to science and want to engage in scientific activities. As with students who join a sports team, the scholar programs require a commitment that raises everyone's game.[6]

3. *Scholar programs are intensive.* The students maintain contact because the peer cohort needs to connect often enough to gel as a team. Over time, the peers feel a strengthened sense of belongingness and a connection to STEM by virtue of their shared venture. Peers can serve as buffers against negative messages society may send about their lack of belonging in the field.[7] Many programs convene members on a weekly or biweekly basis, and many also have prolonged periods of team building as well as training sessions with seasoned peers, professionals, faculty, and staff. New students immersed in a scholar program become connected to many individuals in the STEM community and are more apt to view themselves as part of that community.

4. *Scholar programs are well resourced.* Scholar programs are typically supported by an endowed fund or by grants because they are expensive. Most take place face-to-face on a weekly basis for at least a year or two. Programs often offer a combination of team building, academic training, financial assistance, and research or internship experiences. The program's intensity requires a great investment of financial and human resources for only a select number of students who receive the program's numerous benefits.

Next, I discuss two specific examples of STEM scholar programs, the Posse Scholars program and the Meyerhoff Scholars Program.

Posse Scholars. According to founder Deborah Bial, the premise of this program is that by creating a posse of students who are prepared to succeed and sending them to college with appropriate support, they will be more likely to persist.[8] The following statement from the Posse Foundation website (see posse.org) offers one student's explanation for leaving college: "If I only had my posse with me, I never would have dropped out." Although not exclusively for any particular demographic group, three out of four Posse students are from underrepresented groups, and about two out of three are first-generation college students.

The Posse Scholars selection process is highly competitive for the partner institution and for the students. The foundation is selective about the college or university partner: First the institution must demonstrate that it provides full tuition merit scholarships and an on-site mentor to work with Posse Scholars. Second, the Posse Foundation screens hundreds of student applications, focusing on academic and leadership potential. Of the 20 students who make the cut at an institution, only 10 will be selected for the posse.

Cohort development is very intentional. The Posse Foundation provides the selected students with eight months of training prior to college entrance. For the first two years of college, the scholars meet weekly in a group and biweekly in one-on-one meetings with the on-site mentor and a staff or faculty mentor at the partnering campus. The results are remarkable: Ninety percent of Posse Scholars graduate from a range of prestigious colleges (see posse.org). From day one, Posse Scholars are treated as leaders and are repeatedly told that people believe in their potential for success. Because most Posse Scholars are students of color and first-generation college students, over time, the organization has created a diverse network of alumni.[9]

Building on the Posse Scholars model, Brandeis University launched the first Science Posse Scholars program in 2008, established through a grant from the Howard Hughes Medical Institute and with support from the Posse Foundation (see www.brandeis.edu/acserv/posse/about). Scholars in the Brandeis Science Posse attend a very intensive and effective two-week summer science boot camp and enroll in a math and science course in their first year.[10] Other schools have followed suit with different versions, including Bryn Mawr's all-women's STEM Posse (see news.brynmawr.edu/2012/02/07/posse-announcement).

Meyerhoff Scholars Program. One of the best-known STEM scholar programs is the Meyerhoff Scholars Program at the University of Maryland, Baltimore County, which president and cofounder Freeman Hrabowski has championed. The Meyerhoff Scholars Program has a rigorous selection process and features 13 key components including strong financial support, peer study groups, a required summer bridge program, a shared residential location, professional mentoring, and student attendance at research conferences (see meyerhoff.umbc.edu/13-key-components).

According to multiple published research studies on the program, Meyerhoff Scholars were five times more likely to persist in a STEM major or continue on to graduate school in STEM compared to those who were invited to join the program but attended another university, contributing to a national reputation for producing African American mathematicians and scientists.[11] The Meyerhoff Scholars Program model emphasizes critical mass, demonstrating to the campus that large numbers of racially diverse students can achieve excellence in STEM. Cohorts of Meyerhoff Scholars range from 50 to 60 per year. In addition, because the program includes a dozen other elements such as residential colocation and research participation, the program's intensity and comprehensiveness are greater.

Initiative Highlights

Despite the many positive outcomes associated with a scholar program, not all departments in an institution will choose to pursue this option. Some department heads might decide a scholar program does not match their departmental or institutional values because the program is offered to only a small, select number of students. Some institutions cannot afford all the bells and whistles of the program, or they may not have the mentoring personnel to undertake such an intensive program. The good news is that many different mentoring initiatives can create peer cohorts to enhance belongingness while supporting interest and capacity building during the transition to college.

Toward this peer-focused end, I turn to five types of initiatives a department can implement: course-based communities, residential communities, extended orientations, club-sponsored events, and cascade advising.

Course-based communities. Classrooms can function as communities, such as in first-year seminar programs where students learn together in a small classroom environment and develop organically into a peer cohort.[12] The design and content of introductory courses can help first-year students discover your department and what you have to offer. Duke University experimented with an introduction to forensics as a first-year seminar course.[13] Wellesley College designed an interdisciplinary neuroscience course that combines vision and art, including drawing and painting, problem-based learning, dissecting and other lab exercises, and group work.[14] More campuses are creating introductory premajor classes that get students interested in STEM by integrating a research component.[15]

In some institutions, students can take two courses that are linked by a theme. By integrating STEM into these course-based communities, students can expand their understanding of STEM while also forming closer connections with each other.[16] For example, a student who is initially interested in performance might sign up for a learning community that links a theater course with a course in physics or biology. In addition, many campuses offer an orientation-to-college course that helps students adjust to college.[17] Such courses can be adapted to include sections that are STEM-specific, or transfer student specific, such as a one-credit STEM course for new community college transfer students, which create a peer cohort of students with shared interests and lived experiences.

Each of these introductory course designs that use learning communities can lead students to view a STEM department positively, possibly encouraging a second look at what it has to offer. A course-based approach is advantageous when building a cohort during the academic year. The course can challenge narrow views of STEM while promoting a strong sense of community. In some cases, however, if a learning community becomes too close-knit or intensive, the group may struggle to integrate more fully with other peers at the institution.[18]

Residential communities. Residential communities organize cohorts of students according to shared cocurricular or intellectual interests (e.g., environmental advocacy, engineering and design, health) into common residential living arrangements. These residential arrangements are typically called living-learning communities (LLCs), featuring linked courses, shared residential living spaces, and thematically linked events or projects.[19] By connecting one's discipline to the LLC infrastructure, new students are drawn to discover different fields in a compelling way.[20] For example, women pursuing science who choose a science-focused LLC are more apt to persist in STEM.[21] Despite the promise of residential approaches, some students may feel boxed in and that their academic, social, and living circles are too overlapping and restrictive. In addition, the residential approach is not available to commuting students.

Extended orientations. A summer orientation is a core practice at many four-year institutions; however, the approach to orientation varies widely. In an extended orientation, students engage in some combination of course work, team building, and peer or faculty–staff mentoring to ease the transition into college.[22] Boot camps are orientations that are more intensive or last longer than a typical orientation. They may also be called summer bridge programs, which are even more intense or longer in duration than a boot camp. At Louisiana State University, students are exposed to the rigor of the biology curriculum through an intensive five-day experience that combines sample lectures, learning style assessments, and academic coaching. Data show that ultimately these students earn higher grades than other STEM students who did not choose to enroll.[23] If students benefit from cohort building and skill development before the start of the school year, an extended orientation might be a good choice. However, intensive summer orientations can be difficult for some students to attend if they need the summer weeks for paid work, or if campuses do not have the infrastructure to provide the programming.

Club-sponsored events. Research is still emerging on the benefits of participating in STEM student clubs at the college level.[24] I include clubs as a particular cocurricular activity because they promote regular contact with a range of peers across academic years, in addition to courses or residential experiences. Club-sponsored events provide an on-ramp for students who have yet to take a college STEM course. For example, many clubs host engaging and visible activities that intrigue many students across campus, such as hackathons, design competitions, or speed networking. The Maker Movement, which emphasizes the power of creation while integrating design, the arts, entrepreneurship, and technology, is a powerful attractor for students on many campuses.[25] The shift from STEM to STEAM, emphasizing the integration of the arts and design into STEM as well as the vital role of interdisciplinary collaboration, is closely linked to the Maker Movement.[26]

What Is STEAM?

Putting an *A* in STEM (and using STEAM as a collective acronym) or connecting to the Maker Movement might help you accomplish your department goals (see stemtosteam.org). Consider ways in which your STEM initiatives are connected to the arts, innovation, and design.

Cascade advising. In a cascade advising model, faculty or staff supervise upper-level peer mentors, and those peer mentors advise newer students. Cascade advising can provide a vehicle to improve the initial advising for new students and provide a chance to go beyond courses to broaden students' thinking about what is studied in STEM as well as who studies STEM. Many department administrators who sponsor cascade advising hope for peer mentoring to last the entire semester and may even link new students considering particular majors to upper-level peers in those majors. In many cases, however, the peer advising program is made up of only one or two exchanges because the primary objective is to gain information and new students will have gained what they need from those two encounters. Unless a peer friendship develops, it is unlikely the interactions will persist.

The exchange of information is still very useful, however, so this practice is a worthwhile and often low-cost investment. If peer advisers only have one or two interactions with a new students, it is important to maximize the messages peer advisers deliver and to prepare them to challenge narrow views of STEM curricula and promote interest or engagement in activities. By hiring upper-level students as peer mentors who can provide this initial advising to newer students in their transition to college, you may also succeed in creating a stronger sense of community.

To facilitate access to cascade advising, some campuses use a studio model or a shared space that students can easily locate if they need assistance. Faculty, staff, and peer mentors can hold a portion of their office hours in this space. To pilot this approach, you might try scheduled drop-in hours for peer mentors, along with a rotating schedule for faculty and staff members. Alternatively, peer advisers could be asked to visit first-year seminars or an LLC. Finally, the peer advisers could host events to share their innovative work in the department.

Transition to College: Reader Questions

- How do first-year students discover your major or department?
- Do you have a premajor course? How is that designed?
- Do you have a first-year seminar program?
- Do you have peer advisers?
- Which events do you host, and how do new students learn about them?
- How do students come to know your people, offerings, and spaces?
- Would a studio approach to advising make sense for your department?

Improving the Departmental Climate for New Students

The initiatives described in this chapter can transform the experiences of students, including their own views of themselves, the learning environment, and the reputation of your department. To further explore how climate can be improved for new students, I next focus on the power of role modeling.

Climate is strongly influenced by the presence of diverse, positive role models because role models influence students' sense of belongingness and what is possible for them in STEM.[27] Diverse models may include varying demographic social identities (e.g., race, gender, age) or lived experiences (e.g., family life). Role models may be represented in textbooks, on posters, by the teachers or assistants in our classrooms, by the guests we host, and by the professionals we choose to visit in the workplace.

One strategy is to employ a poster or web campaign that communicates your celebration of diverse role models and, ideally, alumni.[28] A poster campaign will send a positive message as long as the message is consistent with student experiences in classes or in the department spaces (see www.iwitts .org for information on starting a poster campaign). The message would be invalidated if in class students hear disparaging jokes about the incompetence of women or see a department faculty with only one woman or person of color without a clear explanation of how the department is striving to attract diverse staff. There is no point in getting students excited about a department event if no steps have been taken to repair the reputation of a prominent faculty member known for weeding out students in a gateway course. Mixed messages have negative consequences for students and the department as a whole.

Pay attention to how your department's reputation plays a role in student recruitment. Carefully study how and where students, staff, and faculty spend time with one another, whether they are working on course material or engaging in a department event. Many opportunities exist to create and change climate. Remember to start small, and track how your efforts are paying off.

Departmental Climate Ideas: New Students

- Create peer clusters in classes so the women or students of color are not isolated.
- Use bulletin boards to display photos of current majors, alumni, or other successful individuals in the profession representing diverse identities.
- Consider who you select as peer mentors, upper-level research assistants, and graduate teaching assistants. Examine the process for identifying and recruiting them. If you enroll nontraditional-age transfer students, for example, consider whether they are being invited to apply for teaching assistant positions.
- Remember that career panels send important messages to newer students. Think about who is invited to participate on these panels and the messages that are being sent by your selection. If you host other department events, consider the messages these events send to new students who encounter your department for the first time.
- Be aware of the current diversity among your faculty and staff and which faculty or staff are working with students in courses or in clubs. What do students know about your department's commitment to diversity in regard to hiring new faculty and staff?
- Consider ways to infuse energy into STEM classrooms, hallways, and study spaces. New students will see good energy and want to be a part of it.
- Reflect on how connected your department is to STEAM and design.

Case Study: Bill Gomez

In this section, I illustrate the process of designing mentoring initiatives during the transition to college using the case of Bill Gomez, whom we met in the introduction. As this book's focal computer science professor, Gomez teaches at a large, public research university. He has been running a summer program that targets students after their first year of college. Just like the major in computer science, Bill's program consistently enrolls few women, so he wants to change his strategy and enroll students in the program upon their entry to the university. In this case, Bill has chosen to focus on women in computer science and their transition into college.

Step 1: Understand the Factors

Bill begins by asking questions that will help him determine the primary factors influencing students during the transition to college, including the following:

- What percentage of the incoming class at his institution are women? Are the women choosing other STEM majors (just not computer science)?
- How many women enroll in the introductory computer science course? How many of these women go on to become computer science majors?

In his analysis of enrollments in core classes and the number of majors, he finds very few women majoring in computer science—only 24 out of 251, or not quite 10%. Looking even more closely he finds that only 4 of the women are Latina or African American. Institutional data show that women make up 54% of the incoming students, and 22% of those women are Latina or African American. Overall, only about a third of students who enroll in the introductory computer science course convert into majors. He learns that many students who enroll in computer science decide ultimately to continue in statistics, math, or psychology. Bill concludes that there are specific concerns with the recruitment of women students into the introductory course as well as the persistence of women who take that course to declare a computer science major.

Bill also asks the following:

- What do entering students know about careers in STEM fields and, in particular, computer science? Have female students been exposed to cocurricular activities that might encourage STEM enrollment?
- What was the experience of students in the introductory course?
- Do women students report having diverse, positive role models in the computer science field?

TABLE 3.1
Bill's Primary Obstacles and Mentoring Goals

Bill's Primary Obstacles	Bill's Mentoring Goals
Students, particularly female first-years, do not feel a sense of belongingness in computer science.	Increase connections to people in the field by introducing peer cohorts.
Students view the introductory course as challenging but not interesting.	Change the course assignments to be more relevant.
Students lack knowledge about the field, including careers.	Broaden students' knowledge about the field using the course redesign and cascade advising mechanisms.
Students lack role models in computer science but have many in other fields.	Diversify role models in computer science.

To find out students' impressions of the introductory courses and about their knowledge of the field, Bill decides to conduct focus groups with new students at the end of their first year. Let's say that he learns that first-year students overall do not know many people in the computer science field, and they do not perceive that computer science is a community with which they feel connected. Also, students report that the introductory course is very challenging but not very interesting or relevant because of the nature of the assignments. He also learns that women students had more engaging experiences in other courses such as introductions to statistics and psychology. In these settings, they saw greater gender diversity among faculty and students and felt there was greater relevance to course projects. He has identified his primary obstacles and can translate them into goals for his mentoring initiative (see Table 3.1).

Step 2: Choose a Mentoring Strategy

Bill decides a STEM scholar program could work in his department, and he wants to tap into the Maker Movement. Despite being at a large research university, he thinks that a science posse-like experience, such as a smaller gender-balanced cohort of about 10–12 Maker Design scholars, is more feasible given existing resources. Bill can easily fund five or six women students in his summer program right now, but he lacks the women applicants. By reallocating the existing funding, he can try this new approach. He can still offer a coed program, and he will intentionally offer admission-linked scholarships to a peer cohort of women to bring them together during the transition to college.

Bill also proposes a redesigned introductory course to precede the gateway to the major programming course. This new course will include an interactive design component that will intersect with a variety of real-world problems including environmental sustainability and health. As a long-term goal, he wants to explore changing the capstone course. His idea is to eventually form a partnership with a local company on a mutually interesting project in the capstone course.

Finally, he thinks that a cascade advising model could benefit new students. He wants to research the information he would like all new students to know about computer science. He may need more information about existing advising using near-peers (students who have recently taken the course) to decide if integrating what he needs into an existing structure is feasible. Peer advisers could visit students enrolled in a range of first-year seminars to demonstrate some of the activities for students in computer science. He could also host an advising event or try a poster campaign showcasing upper-level students or alumni, noting that he will have to reach back several years or collaborate with a nearby institution to showcase a sufficient number of women.

Step 3: Does This Plan Make Sense?

Bill's initial resource inventory is promising (see Table 3.2). He already has funding for a summer program that he can adapt to support this new initiative. He will need to invest his time in revamping the course or enlist a colleague to join him in this venture, and he will need to hire near-peer advisers. He may also need to see if there is money in the department budget for posters, or if he needs to ask the university communications office for help as part of a larger strategic effort.

Bill's logic model includes targeting a group of entering female (and male) students for a scholar program as well as changing the introductory computer science course and possibly using cascade advising and a poster campaign.

Bill develops the following if/then statements:

- If I change the introductory course to make it more relevant, then I will see more students, including more women, emerging with a stronger interest in taking future computer science courses and wanting to sign up for the summer program.
- If female students are recruited at admission into a Maker Design scholar program, then I will see more women reporting a sense of belongingness and becoming computer science majors.

TABLE 3.2
Bill's Mentoring Strategy and Plan

Mentoring Goals (Outcomes You Hope For)	Activities to Facilitate Mentoring (Programs, Practices, Events)	What Resources Are Needed? (Existing Programs? External Grants?)	How Will You Know If the Initiative Is Successful?
Belongingness	Scholar program, five to six female students at admission	Partners with admissions, leverage existing program funds	Enrollments, reports in first-year focus groups
Relevance of course	Change introductory course project	Bill teaches this course, enlists collaboration with colleague	Course evaluations, subsequent enrollment
Knowledge of field	Cascade advising and intro course	Salary for near-peer advisers	Reports of students after sessions
Diversity models	Poster campaign	Department budget, ask university communication office for help	First-year focus groups

Step 4: Start Small With a Pilot, and Track Progress

Bill may choose to start small by launching the Maker Design scholar program. He may also implement the cascade advising program if the funds and advisers can be easily accessed.

Reader Next Steps: Explore Your Options During the Transition to College

What are your current options in your department? Which ones do you want to explore?

Transition Options

Options	We Have This	I Want to Explore This
Scholar cohort program		
Summer bridge		

(Continues)

Options	We Have This	I Want to Explore This
Cascade advising		
Guest visits or field trips		
Introductory courses or first-year seminar program		
Cocurricular club events		
Residential community		
Teaching assistants linked to courses		
Poster campaign		
Other ideas:		

Your Goals, Activities, Resources, and Indicators

Mentoring Goals (Outcomes You Hope For)	Activities to Facilitate Mentoring (Programs, Practices, Events, Policies)	What Resources Are Needed? (Existing Programs? External Grants?)	How Will You Know If the Initiative Is Successful? (Indicators of Progress)

Your If/Then Statements

If I _____,

then I will see _____.

If _____,

then _____.

Pilot: What would a pilot look like for your initiative(s)?

Tracking: How will you know when your initiative has been successful?

Notes

1. Good, C., Rattan, A., & Dweck, C. S. (2012). Why do women opt out? Sense of belonging and women's representation in mathematics. *Journal of Personality and Social Psychology, 102*(4), 700–717; Ostrove, J. M., & Long, S. M. (2007). Social class and belonging: Implications for college adjustment. *Review of Higher Education, 30*(4), 363–389; Oyserman, D., Brickman, D., Bybee, D., & Celious, A. (2006). Fitting in matters: Markers of in-group belonging and academic outcomes. *Psychological Science, 17*(10), 854–861; Walton, G. M., & Cohen, G. L. (2007). A question of belonging: Race, social fit, and achievement. *Journal of Personality and Social Psychology, 92*(1), 82–96. doi:10.1037/0022-3514.92.1.82

2. Hunn, V. (2014). African American students, retention, and team-based learning: A review of the literature and recommendations for retention at predominantly White institutions. *Journal of Black Studies, 45*(4), 301–314; Stanger-Hall, K., Lang, S., & Maas, M. (2010). Facilitating learning in large lecture classes: Testing the "teaching team" approach to peer learning. *CBE–Life Sciences Education, 9*(4), 489–503.

3. Barlow, E. L., & Villarejo, M. (2004). Making a difference for minorities: Evaluation of an educational enrichment program. *Journal of Research in Science Teaching, 41*(9), 861–881.

4. Aubé, C., Rousseau, V., Tremblay, S. (2011). Team size and quality of group experience: The more the merrier? *Group Dynamics: Theory, Research, and Practice, 15*(4), 357–375.

5. Mueller, J. S. (2011). Why individuals in larger teams perform worse. *Organizational Behavior and Human Decision Processes, 117*(1), 111–124.

6. Hilberg, S., Joshi, A., & House, A. (2009). Washington State Achievers Program: Influence of the scholarship program on low-income college students' achievement and aspirations. *Journal of College Student Retention: Research, Theory & Practice, 10*(4), 447–464; Myers, C. B., & Pavel, M. D. (2011). Underrepresented students in STEM: The transition from undergraduate to graduate programs. *Journal of Diversity in Higher Education, 4*(2), 90–105.

7. Dasgupta, N. (2011). Ingroup experts and peers as social vaccines who inoculate the self-concept: The stereotype inoculation model. *Psychological Inquiry, 22*(4), 231–246.

8. Gee, E. G. (2005). An investment in student diversity. *Trusteeship, 13*(2), 1–4.

9. Bial, D., & Rodriguez, A. (2007). Identifying a diverse student body: Selective college admissions and alternative approaches. *New Directions for Student Services, 118*, 17–30.

10. Gura, T. (2015). A posse on the loose. *HHMI Bulletin, 25*(2). Retrieved from http://www.hhmi.org/bulletin/may-2012/posse-loose

11. For example, see Maton, K. I., Hrabowski, F. A., III, & Schmitt, C. L. (2000). African American college students excelling in the sciences: College and postcollege outcomes in the Meyerhoff Scholars Program. *Journal of Research in Science Teaching, 37*(7), 629–654; Stolle-McAllister, K., Sto Domingo, M. R., &

Carrillo, A. (2011). The Meyerhoff way: How the Meyerhoff scholarship program helps Black students succeed in the sciences. *Journal of Science Education and Technology*, *20*(1), 5–16.

12. Tinto, V. (1997). Classrooms as communities: Exploring the educational character of student persistence. *Journal of Higher Education*, *68*(6), 599–623.

13. Charkoudian, L. K., Heymann, J. J., Adler, M. J., Haas, K. L., Mies, K. A., & Bonk, J. F. (2008). Forensics as a gateway: Promoting undergraduate interest in science and graduate student professional development through a first-year seminar course. *Journal of Chemical Education*, *85*(6), 807–812.

14. Lafer-Sousa, R., & Conway, B. R. (2009). Vision and art: An interdisciplinary approach to neuroscience education. *Journal of Undergraduate Neuroscience Education*, *8*(1), A10–A17.

15. Brownell, S. E., Khalfan, W., Bergmann, D., & Simoni, R. (2013). Explorations: A research-based program introducing undergraduates to diverse biology research topics taught by grad students and postdocs. *Journal of College Science Teaching*, *42*(3), 24–31; Harrison, M., Dunbar, D., Ratmansky, L., Boyd, K., & Lopatto, D. (2011). Classroom-based science research at the introductory level: Changes in career choice and attitude. *CBE–Life Sciences Education*, *10*, 279–286.

16. Tinto, V. (2003). *Learning better together: The impact of learning communities on student success*. Retrieved from http://www.wsac.wa.gov/sites/default/files/2014.ptw.%2855%29.pdf

17. Torres, V., & LePeau, L. (2013). Making the connection: The use of student development theory in first-year and transition programs. *Journal of the First-Year Experience & Students in Transition*, *25*(2), 13–26.

18. Jaffee, D., Carle, A. C., Phillips, R., & Paltoo, L. (2008). Intended and unintended consequences of first-year learning communities: An initial investigation. *Journal of the First-Year Experience & Students in Transition*, *20*(1), 53–70.

19. Wawrzynski, M. R., & Jessup-Anger, J. (2010). From expectations to experiences: Using a structural typology to understand first-year student outcomes in academically based living-learning communities. *Journal of College Student Development*, *51*(2), 201–217.

20. Rohli, R. V., & Rogge, R. A. (2012). An empirical study of the potential for geography in university living-learning communities in the United States. *Journal of Geography in Higher Education*, *36*(1), 81–95.

21. Szelenyi, K., & Inkelas, K. K. (2011). The role of living-learning programs in women's plans to attend graduate school in STEM fields. *Research in Higher Education*, *52*(4), 349–369; Whalen, D. F., & Shelley, M. C. (2010). Academic success for STEM and non-STEM majors. *Journal of STEM Education: Innovations and Research*, *11*(1/2), 45–60.

22. Contreras, F. (2011). Strengthening the bridge to higher education for academically promising underrepresented students. *Journal of Advanced Academics*, *22*(3), 500–526.

23. Wischusen, S. M., & Wischusen, E. W. (2007). Biology intensive orientation for students (BIOS): A biology "boot camp." *CBE–Life Sciences Education, 6*(2) 172–178.

24. Gottfried, M. A., & Williams, D. (2013). STEM club participation and STEM schooling outcomes. *Education Policy Analysis Archives, 21*(79). Retrieved from epaa.asu.edu/ojs/article/view/1361

25. Halverson, E. R., & Sheridan, K. M. (2014). The Maker Movement in education. *Harvard Educational Review, 84*(4), 495–504.

26. Guyotte, K. W., Sochacka, N. W., Constantino, T. E., Walther, J., & Kellam, N. N. (2014, November). STEAM as social practice: Cultivating creativity in transdisciplinary spaces. *Art Education,* 13–19.

27. Scandura, T. A., & Williams, E. A. (2001). An investigation of the moderating effects of gender on the relationships between mentorship initiation and protégé perceptions of mentoring functions. *Journal of Vocational Behavior, 59,* 342–363.

28. Cheryan, S., Plaut, V. C., Davies, P. G., & Steele, C. M. (2009). Ambient belonging: How stereotypical cues impact gender participation in computer science. *Journal of Personality and Social Psychology, 97*(6), 1045–1060. doi:10.1037/a0016239

4

WHAT WORKS (AND WHY) DURING THE TRANSITION TO A STEM MAJOR

During the transition to a STEM major, we can see that the factors of capacity, interest, and belongingness play an important role. Your department has the opportunity to create an environment where students from a wide range of backgrounds can thrive in STEM. Students are comparing prospective majors, and what the department does to actively invite students in and support them will make a difference in persistence.

In this chapter, I emphasize the capacity to learn because of the centrality of gateway courses when students consider the prospect of a STEM major. Will students view the courses as serving a *gatekeeper* function, keeping them away from the major? Learning environments need to support the development of problem-solving skills, rather than weed out students while they strive to learn. Research experiences build confidence when students engage in difficult problems, whether the research takes place in the summer, in a course, or through a work-study or part-time job during the academic term. When students experience success and receive timely feedback and messages encouraging them to persist, they are more likely to emerge feeling capable and that they belong in the STEM community.

Student interest can be reinforced by highlighting the relevance of what they are learning to the real world. In addition, belongingness can be influenced by promoting peer learning. Finally, the departmental climate plays a role through the messages the department sends regarding learning and belongingness. Students form a positive impression when they hear messages that students can increase their skills (rather than messages saying they can't) and when they perceive that the faculty, staff, and student support staff are approachable.

The Transition to a STEM Major: Questions Students Ask

- Do I fit in this major?
- Are the STEM gateway courses and cocurricular activities interesting to me?
- Can I be successful in these STEM courses?
- Do I feel confident that I can solve difficult problems? Am I getting a lot of practice?
- Am I engaging in research?
- Do I see the relevance of what I am learning to the world around me?
- Does peer collaboration happen in class as well as outside class?
- Are people who are like me valued here and specifically in STEM spaces?
- Does this department have communal learning spaces where I want to spend time?

What Works and Why

In this next section, I spotlight STEM summer research mentoring programs as a promising approach that addresses the three factors of capacity, interest, and belongingness and impacts students during their transition to a STEM major. After participating in effective summer research programs, many students decide a STEM major or career is for them. Even if you are familiar with summer research, I suggest you examine the details of the two programs discussed here. These examples provide far more integration with academic success in gateway courses than is typical in the standard summer research program. In addition, many alternative initiatives exist, requiring different types of resources and levels of intensity.

Spotlight: STEM Summer Research Mentoring Programs

A promising approach to motivating students to embark on a STEM major is a summer science research program.[1] Like STEM scholar mentoring programs (discussed in Chapter 3), many summer science research programs refer to their participants as *scholars*. Most summer research programs take place after the first year of college, which is different from other scholar programs. Summer research programs reinforce the importance of problem-solving skills and motivate students to persist in gateway courses.

Research shows the effectiveness of summer science research mentoring programs in promoting learning in STEM, persistence in STEM majors, or increased commitment to graduate study, particularly among members of underrepresented groups.[2] Students who engage in undergraduate research are more likely to pursue upper-level course work and persist in the major than students who do not engage in undergraduate research.[3] Participation in summer research supports the strong development of *self-efficacy*, defined as confidence in one's ability to achieve in a given domain.[4]

Over the past decade, we have discovered the following four elements that outline how summer research experiences promote persistence in the major by connecting students to the science community:

1. *Students work closely with seasoned professionals* in structured apprenticeships where they gain new knowledge, hone their skills, and develop identities in the field as part of a larger community of researchers.[5] By being involved in the craft of the field, students often learn more about what they need to learn in the field and why.

2. *Students gain learning strategies to use in gateway courses.* Research is not the students' only takeaway from a summer experience. When students receive academic coaching on metacognition, they can take a step back, strategize about what they are learning and how, and are empowered to persist.[6]

3. *Newer students participate in the research.* While once reserved for upper-level students, research experiences are now recognized as a high-impact practice for newer students because they increase students' confidence and retention in college.[7] Although newer students do not have the same course work as seasoned students, they are typically supervised by upper-level students and, as a result, become connected to a community of students.[8] Research experiences that start early in a student's academic career can play a critical role in helping the student develop an interest in STEM fields by providing real-world views and hands-on experiences.[9] A multiyear approach to research also means more sophomores and juniors will have an opportunity to gain a second summer or year of experience and take on a leadership role as a peer mentor in the lab.[10]

4. *Students experience intensity in the programs.* Many resources are channeled into a high-quality experience for a small number of students that require significant faculty time and funding. As a result, the programs are intensive and necessarily expensive, typically funded by a federal grant or an endowed fund. Many campuses have their own version of a summer research program, such as a research experience

for undergraduates sponsored by the National Science Foundation, a consortia model (e.g., Summer Research Opportunity Program available via the Committee on Institutional Cooperation; see www.cic.net/students/srop/introduction), a national model (e.g., Mellon Mays Undergraduate Fellows Program; see www.mmuf.org), or an, endowed program particular to your institution.

Here I discuss two examples, Louisiana State University's LA-STEM Research Scholars Program and the University of California, Davis's Biology Undergraduate Scholars Program (BUSP), both of which emphasize summer science research and strategies needed to tackle learning in gateway courses.

LA-STEM. Louisiana State University's LA-STEM, funded by the Howard Hughes Medical Institute and created by Isaiah Warner, uses a model that provides scholars with challenging research opportunities, a mentoring team, and academic support workshops that include an emphasis on metacognitive learning strategies.[11] Students engage in self-assessments followed by targeted advice from faculty, thereby helping students change their learning strategies.

In LA-STEM, first- and second-year students who are selected to participate have demonstrated underperformance in their first year but have also shown potential to improve. Impressively, program participants graduate with STEM degrees an average of 20 percentage points higher than comparable students not in the program. In addition, half of the participants are African American who graduate at nearly the same rate in STEM as White participants—a stark contrast to nationwide trends showing large racial achievement gaps. The program emphasizes the need for students to uncover and repair unproductive learning patterns, commit to a change in mind-set, and be willing to try new strategies. Concurrently, students join a research lab, and the combination leads to thriving in the field.

BUSP. Students in this program benefit from paid employment in research laboratories as well as strengthened advising in STEM. The program emphasizes participation in peer-led facilitated study groups (described more fully later in this in chapter) for calculus, biology, and chemistry.[12] The combination of learning strategy workshops among peers and socialization in lab settings cultivates stronger academic and career peer support.[13] While the program originally focused on recruiting students of color, the pool of students has broadened to include first-generation college students from all racial backgrounds. These students demonstrate much better outcomes: BUSP scholars are two to three times more likely than control students to complete their math and science courses and pursue graduate study. BUSP program results also suggest that early research experiences during the first two years and the pursuit of research for more than one semester are predictive of improved student persistence and long-term positive career outcomes.[14]

Initiative Highlights

Despite the many positive outcomes associated with a summer research program, not all department administrators decide to pursue this option. They may wish to provide access with less commitment on the part of the student or the research mentor, involve many more students, or use a combination of academic year and summer strategies. Fortunately, an intensive summer program is not the only vehicle for benefitting from research exposure; many campuses have access to a range of course-based mechanisms to provide research experience.

In this section, I highlight course-based approaches to gaining research experience that also integrate career-relevant messages. Then I discuss the ways courses can be improved by emphasizing active learning with quality feedback, incorporating peer-led academic instruction, or providing booster modules targeting requisite skills.

Course-based approaches to gaining research experience. Offering research experience as a course can be very effective in student persistence because the approach can incorporate elements similar to those in summer research programs. Many departments have a research course at the upper level but fewer involve research at an earlier, but also highly beneficial, stage.[15] One positive aspect of embedding research within courses is that an integrated course approach can provide research opportunities to more students.[16] At the University of Hawaii, the C-MORE program is a great example of providing students with powerful research lab experience during the academic year.[17] Course-based models are especially promising when lab space or research financial support are not as available. In addition, faculty are compensated for course-based commitments, obviating the need for extra compensation for summer research.[18] Currently, many courses that integrate research do so by having students run prepared experiments that teach particular concepts but are not necessarily linked to authentic research. Embedding authentic research into a course by connecting to a professor's own line of research (e.g., an inquiry into genomes) has definitively demonstrated increased student learning, confidence, and interest in pursuing future research.[19]

Integrating career-relevant messages in courses. Beyond engaging in research, there are many models for communicating career-relevant messages in courses. Some departments integrate their core biology, chemistry, and physics courses into combined interdisciplinary sequences.[20] In other cases, instructors use MIT's open source website (see ocw.mit.edu/index.htm) to integrate interdiscplinary examples into lessons. These additions do not impose on normal instruction, often totalling about five minutes a week.[21] In addition, ENGAGE in Engineering, a National Science Foundation project, has a bank of everyday examples of engineering that faculty can use to illustrate and drive home concepts (see www.engageengineering.org/e3s). Alternatively, departments can establish the relevance of course work by bringing students to professionals in their workplaces or inviting professionals to be guests in class activities. For example, an instructor or department can include guests, either in person or through videoconferencing, as participants in courses, career panels, fireside chats, or coffee hours. Another way to integrate career-relevant messages is for the professor to spend a minute on a career profile as part of class discussion, akin to a daily news feature. Faculty can also use this approach to reach many students by embedding short advising messages about the STEM career path into their lessons on a regular basis.[22]

Career relevance may "hook" the student, but for longterm success in those careers, students need instruction that will support their conceptual understanding and long-term retention of material. Toward that end, courses need to emphasize active learning with quality feedback, incorporate peer-led academic support, or provide booster modules.

Active learning with quality feedback. Students taking gateway courses require consistent, timely feedback as well as chances to practice skills and improve self-efficacy. Substantial failure rates are the norm in introduction or gateway courses. The evidence suggests gateway courses could be structured more effectively.[23] Lectures can be combined with student-centered inquiry to promote lasting conceptual understanding.[24] Students need chances to engage with the material, ask questions, synthesize their learning, and deepen their understanding.[25] These processes are more likely to occur when students can practice frequently (rather than perform only one time, such as on a final exam) and receive quick, regular feedback through peer debate on a daily or weekly basis.[26]

Formative assessment provides students with opportunities to check their understanding as they go along rather than waiting to find out what they do or do not know during a high-stakes midterm or final exam. Formative assessment helps more than just the students: When structured well, the professor and teaching assistants learn what to emphasize during instruction.[27] For example, instructors can incorporate preclass reading quizzes or in-class questions with students using clickers to check for comprehension or to promote discussion.[28] Faculty can use other active learning exercises (minute papers, case studies, sample exam questions with discussion, etc.) that enhance comprehension and engagement.[29]

Feedback can also take the form of demonstrating learning processes, such as how to read the research literature effectively or discussing the steps involved in problem solving.[30] More faculty are using online office hours with technology such as Google Hangouts or posting a short video or audio file for the class to clear up students' misapprehension about a concept revealed in homework they turned in.[31] Many of these strategies have been shown to reduce attrition, particularly among learners from diverse backgrounds.[32]

Peer-led academic support. Beyond feedback from faculty, research documents strong benefits in peer-led academic support, particularly peer-led support in gateway courses. Near-peers are students who have taken the course and can promote the practice of problem solving in a proactive and community-oriented fashion. Although access to traditional tutoring is important, tutoring as an approach presents some drawbacks; for example, students must first struggle and then identify themselves as needing additional support. Research supports the notion that particular habits of mind, such as collaborative learning and problem solving, lead to success in STEM fields. When near-peer academic mentors lead collective problem-solving sessions for all students enrolled in the course, all students can deepen their learning, not just those who are struggling.[33] Ultimately, an investment in near-peer mentoring is cost-effective for institutions in terms of saving faculty's time (i.e., reduce requests for appointments or lines for help during office hours) and improving students' success. With these programs in place, you also have a ready-made crew of peer mentors with academic strengths whose mentoring in one realm can often be applied in other realms, such as navigation of the major or socioemotional support. Now, we discuss four typical formats for delivering near-peer academic support.

In supplemental instruction (SI), near-peer instructors lead sessions with prepared interactive workshop materials and intentionally head off trouble spots rather than waiting for students in the course to generate questions. The peer instructor often provides a repeat of the professor's lecture focusing on what the students found confusing. Attendance at the SI session is encouraged for all students, not just for those seeking remediation. Accordingly, a wide array of students participate, representing a range of prior experiences and degrees of competency. Students who attend SI sessions demonstrate improved grades and retention in the major.[34] The University of Missouri-Kansas City's International Center for Supplemental Instruction features resources for more information (see www.umkc.edu/asm/si/index.shtml).

Similar to SI sessions, a facilitated study group (FSG) encourages excellence for all students by organizing a learning setting for students to cooperatively practice the skills that students in prior classes found the most difficult. The method was made popular by Phillip Uri Treisman, an American mathematician and professor, who noted that certain under-represented students tended to study alone with detrimental outcomes, while majority students benefited from regular study group sessions in which they practiced problem solving.[35] The FSG emphasizes collaborative problem solving rather than a repeat of the lecture. In the session, the FSG peer leader facilitates problem-solving exercises to promote effective studying. As with the SI approach, the students do not need to search for a peer study group or raise their hand to ask for help. The underlying premise is that students learn better when they work together rather than alone. In practice, SI and FSG elements can be used to complement each other; FSG sessions begin with a mini lecture similar to that found in SI sessions, and many SI sessions, conclude with an FSG-like practice session. Department administrators should consider whether and how to alter their tutoring services to include SI or FSG sessions for gateway courses.

In some STEM fields, the SI and FSG models do not make as much sense as open lab or studio models. For example, in computer science, open lab support occurs when near-peers offer students help with debugging their code or provide more sophisticated peer code review sessions where near-peers read students' code and offer feedback.[36] In mathematics, this open lab session is sometimes called a studio model. The studio is just another name for a common study space, typically converted from a lounge or class-room space. In the studio, near-peers (and instructors alike) are on call, and students know where they can go to work and get help when they need it (e.g., see Greenfield Community College's math studio at www.gcc.mass.edu/math/studio).

Another option is to add a fourth-hour workshop to a course where that time period can be used for peer-led workshops.[37] In this model, the peer-led workshops become a fundamental part of how students are taught and how they learn. This approach also encourages attendance because the workshops are part of the class schedule rather than, say, an optional component in the evening when not all students can be there.

If departments struggle with a minimal student employment budget, a professor could choose to structure peer learning groups into existing lab sessions or try to offer their own office hours in an open lab or studio model. All these peer and near-peer options help build community while students participate in STEM course work.

Modules that boost requisite skills. Although peer-led academic support sessions can be very helpful in supporting most of your students, there are still cases when students lack requisite skills to such a degree that they cannot fully participate. In these cases, peer-led approaches can be limited in their effectiveness, and individual tutorials are not cost-effective. Departments may turn instead to creating modules that boost requisite skills rather than turning students away from their majors or enrolling them in core courses they are likely to fail. When students lack the skills to complete core requisites successfully, they often are deterred from declaring a STEM major.[38] Remediation can be successfully accomplished through precourses or through course modules that allow students to make a successful transition into a STEM major.

For example, the Biology Fellows Program at the University of Washington, which is modeled after LA-STEM and other bridge programs, features metacognitive, disciplinary-based workshops in a course designed for premajors to allow students to build their skills before they begin the gateway course.[39] In addition, ENGAGE Engineering (engageengineering.org) provides information about a range of engineering programs that screen for prerequisite skills and provide booster modules if necessary. For example, universities screen for spatial-visualization skills in students who want to study engineering. If the results are not positive, they provide students with access to a booster module of spatial relations, rather than summarily blocking entrance to the major. This approach fosters an inclusive environment, which positively affects persistence.[40]

If you do not have these course modules available, I recommend you discuss the feasibility of developing them, perhaps by talking to someone at a peer institution who has developed and implemented them with success. You can then decide if investing in such an option would align with your department's goals.

Transition Into a STEM Major: Reader Questions

- How do prospective majors experience your gateway courses?
- Do you screen for requisite skills? Is there a mechanism that allows students to make the transition into the major through a booster module in that requisite skill?
- Do students have access to regular feedback in classes?
- Is peer-led academic instruction the norm for your gateway courses?

Improving Departmental Climate for Prospective and Current Majors

This chapter emphasizes how the learning environment can influence student recruitment and persistence during the transition into a STEM major. We can see how climate contributes to the learning environment. Having a growth mind-set ethos in the department can influence persistence because such beliefs have a bearing on how instructors and students engage in skill development. A discussion of growth mind-set, first among colleagues at the department level and then with your students, can help students persist and more actively seek help for their learning and encourage instructors to try alternatives, whether active learning, peer support, or a booster module targeting requisite skills.[41] A department-level discussion about and explicit teaching of metacognitive learning strategies can also be effective. Countless students expend many hours preparing for class and completing assignments without using those hours effectively.[42] A department's reputation is not just about what people believe, however; it is also about resources. Will you allocate resources so that students can gain requisite skills or practice problem solving as a communal activity? Will you allocate resources so faculty and staff can participate in a workshop to try new strategies?

We know negative stereotypes exist, and their very presence can create anxiety in performance situations. The use of values-affirmation interventions, enacted as a brief writing exercise in which students affirm their values and strengths, have been promising for neutralizing a stereotype threat by bolstering identity in other areas.[43] This seemingly simple act can have powerful consequences on grades and academic success in the long term.[44] Similar results have been found for reducing the achievement gap for first-generation college students in an introductory gateway biology course.[45] Alternatively, instructors can create an identity-safe environment by recognizing cues in the environment such as cultural- and gender-inclusive language (i.e., not using masculine pronouns for all examples).[46] In addition, the policies you have in place, such as reserving copies of books at the library for students who cannot afford them without waiting to be asked to do so, can send positive identity-inclusive messages. Promoting identity safety does not mean sacrificing rigor; instead, identity safety means sending messages that diverse identities are recognized and welcome in your department.

Finally, in regard to representation, consider carefully the people you invite to campus as well as the examples you provide in class; each of these acts sends a message regarding who belongs in your environment. These messages are most visible in our communal spaces (e.g., a studio space) or in our classrooms as well as in the structure of our curriculum. For example, the visuals in the environment contribute to collective messages, such

---

Departmental Climate Ideas: New and Prospective STEM Majors

- Does your department have a reputation for weeding out students?
- Consider the messages sent by the structure of your curriculum and the feedback provided by faculty, staff, and student support staff. Are you working on talent identification or on talent development?
- Consider which students get invited to serve as peer mentors, upper-level research assistants, and graduate teaching assistants. If you enroll nontraditional-age transfer students, for example, think about whether they are included.
- Consider ways to create relevance in courses through connections to professionals. Think about who is invited to participate in activities at your institution and the messages they send while they are there.
- What do your classrooms, hallways, and study spaces communicate about the energy of your department?

---

as displaying only science fiction posters or only photos of White men as award-winning role models.[47]

Case Study: Susan Mason

In this section, I illustrate the process of designing mentoring initiatives during the transition to a STEM major using the case of Susan Mason, this book's composite chemistry professor who teaches at a private liberal arts college. She wants to improve the persistence of students of color who enroll in Chemistry 1. Many fail to continue on to Chemistry 2, which is required for the major. In this case, Susan has chosen to focus on students of color and the gateway courses in chemistry.

Step 1: Understand the Factors

Susan starts by asking a series of questions to help her determine the primary obstacles influencing persistence during the transition into a chemistry major. She has already identified the first chemistry course as a gateway course and asks herself the following:

- Who is enrolling in Chemistry 1 and Chemistry 2?
- How did students of color perform academically in the first and second chemistry courses?

TABLE 4.1

Susan's Primary Obstacles and Mentoring Goals

Susan's Primary Obstacles	Susan's Mentoring Goals
Students report that Chemistry 1 is academically unsupportive.	Improve perceptions of academic support in this class.
Students find faculty unapproachable.	Improve students' access to faculty.
Students of color perceive a chilly departmental climate from the lack of faculty of color and lack of majors of color.	Increase positive reports of departmental climate from students of color and learn more about professionals and majors of color.

By looking at enrollment data, Susan finds that 120 of the 500 incoming students are taking Chemistry 1. She also finds that 29 of the 120, or nearly 25%, are students of color, mirroring the percentage of students of color at the institution overall. Yet only 50 students are advancing to the next course in the major, and of these 50 students, only 7 are students of color. While some attrition is expected, Susan is concerned about the large number of students who do not convert to majors and also about the disproportionate loss of students of color.

Susan wants to find out about the students experiences in the Chemistry 1 class. Susan contacts her institutional research office for information to help her analyze themes from the end-of-course evaluations from Chemistry 1. Overall, students consistently complain about the large number of students enrolled in the course. They do not feel they are able to access academic support, and they feel that the course is set up for students to sink or swim. The rating "felt supported academically" was consistently rated lower by students of color than by White students. Students who did not advance achieved modestly lower grades than students who did advance, but there were no differences based on race.

Senior surveys collected by the institution reveal additional insights: Seniors of color commented on a chilly climate in the chemistry department, underscored by a lack of racial diversity among the faculty and the lack of a critical mass of students of color who are majors. Students of color wonder about the faculty's commitment to students of color and do not feel faculty are approachable in courses or during office hours. Susan has an initial grasp of what the obstacles are for her students and translates them into a set of mentoring goals (see Table 4.1).

Step 2: Choose a Mentoring Strategy

Susan wants to add FSGs to the Chemistry 1 and 2 sequence. An intentional allocation of resources will help improve academic support and help provide a crew of peer mentors. She also encourages her colleagues to try a studio approach to office hours and use Google Hangouts for a small but important group of commuting students. To provide regular feedback, she incorporates clicker questions and minute papers in class. In addition, she incorporates two-minute interdisciplinary examples into lessons each week.

Finally, Susan wants to determine whether the students in the gateway courses have already accessed research-based experiences. If not, she may look carefully at the college's summer research program and also see if there is a way to target students enrolled in Chemistry 1 to recruit students who have potential but underperformed (similar to LA-STEM).

Step 3: Does This Plan Make Sense?

The good news is that Susan already has access to tutoring funds from her department for use in Chemistry 1 that she plans to reallocate toward the FSG model. She is also able to apply through her dean for a pedagogy innovation grant to pilot test the use of an additional three to four peer mentors for this particular course and a graduate student coordinator for about five hours per week (see Table 4.2). Susan will likely need to enlist an assessment or evaluation partner—in this case, possibly her institutional research office.

TABLE 4.2
Susan's Mentoring Strategy and Plan

Mentoring Goals (Outcomes You Hope For)	Activities to Facilitate Mentoring (Programs, Practices, Events)	What Resources Are Needed? (Existing Programs? External Grants?)	How Will You Know If the Initiative Is Successful? (Indicators of Progress)
Belongingness	Peer-led FSGs	Peer mentors and graduate student coordinator	Attendance and evaluation of sessions
Relevance of course	Active learning promotion	Faculty learning community focused on active learning, money for lunches	Course evaluations, subsequent enrollment
Warmer climate	Studio model of office hours, integration of career messages in class	Colleagues willing to reallocate office hours, time to look for examples or organize visitors	Focus groups for first-year students and graduating majors

Susan's logic model targets Chemistry 1 as well as Chemistry 2. She may need to work with the instructors (fortunately, she is one of them) and the academic support services staff.

Susan's if/then statements are the following:

- If I change the experience in Chemistry 1 and 2 so that it is more supportive of students, then I will see more students, including more students of color, continuing into the chemistry major.
- If I am able to recruit colleagues to engage in active learning, then colleagues will see course evaluations that demonstrate student learning and enhanced confidence.

Step 4: Start Small With a Pilot, and Track Progress

Susan may choose to start small by focusing on Chemistry 1 and forming partnerships with the other instructors of this course as a starting point. She can then focus her energies on academic resources, teaching approaches, use of office hours, and guest speakers for the course. This would limit the amount of additional funds she needs to seek and the number of people she needs to involve to get started.

Reader Next Steps: Explore Your Options During the Transition to a STEM Major

Which models do you already have in your department? Which ones do you want to explore?

Transition Options

Initiative Type	We Have This	I Want to Explore This
Summer research		
Work study		
Research courses		
Metacognition workshops		
Active learning initiatives (clickers, formative assessment)		
Peer-led academic instruction		
Studio model for office hours		
Guests in courses		
Other ideas:		

Your Goals, Activities, Resources, and Indicators

Mentoring Goals (Outcomes You Hope For)	Activities to Facilitate Mentoring (Programs, Practices, Events)	What Resources Are Needed? (Existing Programs? External Grants?)	How Will You Know If the Initiative Is Successful? (Indicators of Progress)

Your If/Then Statements

If I _____,

then _____.

If _____,

then _____.

Pilot: What would a pilot look like for your initiative(s)?

Tracking: How will you know when your initiative has been successful?

Notes

1. Seymour, E., Hunter, A., Laursen, S. L., & DeAntoni, T. (2007). Establishing the benefits of research experiences for undergraduates in the sciences: First findings from a three-year study. *Science Education, 88*(4), 493–534.

2. Jones, M. T., Barlow, A. E. L., & Villarejo, M. (2010). Importance of undergraduate research for minority persistence and achievement in biology. *Journal of Higher Education, 81*(1), 82–115; Slovacek, S., Whittinghill, J., Flenoury, L., & Wiseman, D. (2012). Promoting minority success in the sciences: The minority opportunities in research programs at CSULA. *Journal of Research in Science Teaching, 49*(2), 199–217.

3. Hunter, A., Laursen, S. L., & Seymour, E. (2007). Becoming a scientist: The role of undergraduate research in students' cognitive, personal, and professional development. *Science Education, 91*(1), 36–74.

4. Adedokun, O. A., Bessenbacher, A. B., Parker, L. C., Kirkham, L. L., & Burgess, W. D. (2013). Research skills and STEM undergraduate research students' aspirations for research careers: Mediating effects of research self-efficacy. *Journal of Research in Science Teaching, 50*(8), 940–951.

5. Hunter, A., Laursen, S. L., & Seymour, E. (2007). Becoming a scientist: The role of undergraduate research in students' cognitive, personal, and professional development. *Science Education, 91*(1), 36–74.

6. Wilson, Z., Holmes, L., deGravelles, K., Sylvain, M., Batiste, L., Johnson, M., . . . Warner, I. (2012). Hierarchical mentoring: A transformative strategy for improving diversity and retention in undergraduate STEM disciplines. *Journal of Science Education & Technology, 21*(1), 148–156.

7. Grabowski, J. J., Heely, M. E., & Brindley, J. A. (2008). Scaffolding faculty-mentored authentic research experiences for first-year students. *Council on Undergraduate Research Quarterly, 29*(1), 41–47.

8. Edgcomb, M. R., Crowe, H. A., Rice, J. D., Morris, S. J., Wolffe, R. J., & McConnaughay, K. D. (2010). Peer and near-peer mentoring: Enhancing learning in summer research programs. *Council on Undergraduate Research Quarterly, 31*(2), 18–25.

9. Harrison, M., Dunbar, D., Ratmansky, L., Boyd, K., & Lopatto, D. (2011). Classroom-based science research at the introductory level: Changes in career choices and attitude. *CBE–Life Sciences Education, 10*(3), 279–286.

10. Packard, B. W., Marciano, V., Payne, J. M., Bledzki, L. A., & Woodard, C. T. (2014). Negotiating peer mentoring roles in undergraduate research lab settings. *Mentoring & Tutoring: Partnerships in Learning, 22*(5), 433–445.

11. Wilson, Z., Holmes, L., deGravelles, K., Sylvain, M., Batiste, L., Johnson, M., . . . Warner, I. (2012). Hierarchical mentoring: A transformative strategy for improving diversity and retention in undergraduate STEM disciplines. *Journal of Science Education & Technology, 21*(1), 148–156.

12. Treisman, U. (1992). Studying students studying calculus: A look at the lives of minority mathematics students in college. *College Mathematics Journal, 23*(5), 362–372.

13. Barlow, A. E. L., & Villarejo, M. (2004). Making a difference for minorities: Evaluation of an educational enrichment program. *Journal of Research in Science Teaching, 41*(9), 861–881.

14. Jones, M. T., Barlow, A. E. L., & Villarejo, M. (2010). Importance of undergraduate research for minority persistence and achievement in biology. *Journal of Higher Education, 81*(1), 82–115.

15. Behar-Horenstein, L., & Johnson, M. L. (2010). Enticing students to enter into undergraduate research: The instrumentality of an undergraduate course. *Journal of College Science Teaching, 39*(3), 62–70.

16. Rogers, D. L., Kranz, P. L., & Ferguson, C. J. (2012). The embedded researcher method for involving undergraduates in research: New data and observations. *Journal of Hispanic Higher Education, 12*(3), 225–236.

17. Gibson, B. A., & Bruno, B. C. (2012). The C-MORE scholars program: Motivations for an academic-year research experiences for undergraduates program. *Journal of College Science Teaching, 43*(5), 12–18.

18. Hirst, R., Bolduc, G., Liotta, L., & Packard, B. W. (2014). Cultivating the STEM transfer pathway and capacity for research: A partnership between a community college and a four-year college. *Journal of College Science Teaching, 43*(4), 18–23.

19. Burnette, J. M., III, & Wessler, S. R. (2013). Transposing from the laboratory to the classroom to generate authentic research experiences for undergraduates. *Genetics, 193*(2), 367–375. doi:10.1534/genetics.112.147355

20. Copp, N. H., Black, K., & Gould, S. (2012). Accelerated integrated science sequence: An interdisciplinary introductory course for science majors. *Journal of Undergraduate Neuroscience Education, 11*(1), A76–A81.

21. Vogel Taylor, E. M., Mitchell, R., & Drennan, C. L. (2009). Creating an interdisciplinary introductory chemistry course without time-intensive curriculum changes. *ACS Chemical Biology, 4*(12), 979–982.

22. Packard, B. W., Tuladhar, C., & Lee, J. (2013). Advising in the classroom: How community college STEM faculty support transfer-bound students. *Journal of College Science Teaching, 42*(4), 54–60.

23. Freeman, S., Haak, D., & Wenderoth, M. P. (2011). Increased course structure improves performance in introductory biology. *CBE–Life Sciences Education, 10*(2), 175–186.

24. Derting, T. L., & Ebert-May, D. (2010). Learner-centered inquiry in undergraduate biology: Positive relationships with long-term student achievement. *CBE–Life Sciences Education, 9*(4), 462–472.

25. Crowe, A., Dirks, C., & Wenderoth, M. P. (2008). Biology in bloom: Implementing Bloom's taxonomy to enhance student learning in biology. *CBE–Life Sciences Education, 7*(4), 368–381.

26. Mazur, E. (1997). *Peer instruction: A user's manual.* Upper Saddle River, NJ: Prentice Hall.

27. Eddy, S. L., & Hogan, K. A. (2014). Getting under the hood: How and for whom does increasing course structure work? *CBE–Life Sciences Education, 13*(3), 453–468; Freeman, S., Haak, D., & Wenderoth, M. P. (2011). Increased course

structure improves performance in introductory biology. *CBE–Life Sciences Education, 10*(2), 175–186.

28. Crossgrove, K., & Curran, K. L. (2008). Using clickers in nonmajors and majors-level biology courses: Student opinion, learning, and long-term retention of course material. *CBE–Life Sciences Education, 7*(1), 146–154.

29. Stevens, L. M., & Hoskins, S. G. (2014). The CREATE strategy for intensive analysis of primary literature can be used effectively by newly trained faculty to produce multiple gains in diverse students. *CBE–Life Sciences Education, 12*(2), 224–242.

30. Dirks, C., & Cunningham, M. (2006). Enhancing diversity in science: Is teaching science process skills the answer? *CBE–Life Sciences Education, 5*(3), 218–226.

31. Bowen, J. A. (2012). *Teaching naked: How moving technology out of your classroom will improve student learning.* San Francisco, CA: Jossey-Bass.

32. Haak, D. C., HilleRisLambers, J., Pitre, E., & Freeman, S. (2011). Increased structure and active learning reduce the achievement gap in introductory biology. *Science, 332*(6034), 1213–1216.

33. Fullilove, R. E., & Treisman, P. U. (1990). Mathematics achievement among African American undergraduates at the University of California, Berkeley: An evaluation of the mathematics workshop program. *Journal of Negro Education, 59*(3), 463–478.

34. Blanc, R. A., DeBuhr, L. E., & Martin, D. C. (1983). Breaking the attrition cycle: The effects of supplemental instruction on undergraduate performance and attrition. *Journal of Higher Education, 54*(1), 80–90; Congos, D. H., Langsam, D. M., & Schoeps, N. (1997). Supplemental instruction: A successful approach to learning how to learn college introductory biology. *Journal of Teaching and Learning, 2*(1), 2–17; Peterfreund, A. R., Rath, K. A., Xenos, S. P., & Bayliss, F. (2008). The impact of supplemental instruction on students in STEM courses: Results from San Francisco State University. *Journal of College Student Retention: Research, Theory & Practice, 9*(4), 487–503; Rath, K. A., Peterfreund, A. R., Xenos, S. P., Bayliss, F., & Carnal, N. (2007). Supplemental instruction in introductory biology I: Enhancing the performance and retention of underrepresented minority students. *CBE–Life Sciences Education, 6*(3), 203–216.

35. Fullilove, R. E., & Treisman, P. U. (1990). Mathematics achievement among African American undergraduates at the University of California, Berkeley: An evaluation of the mathematics workshop program. *Journal of Negro Education, 59*(3), 463–478.

36. Wang, Y., Hang, L., Feng, Y., Jiang, Y., & Liu, Y. (2012). Assessment of programming language learning based on peer code review model: Implementation and experience report. *Computers & Education, 59*(2), 412–422.

37. Preszler, R. W. (2009). Replacing lecture with peer-led workshops improves student learning. *CBE- Life Sciences Education, 8* (Fall), 182–192.

38. Bailey, T. (2009). Challenge and opportunity: Rethinking the role and function of developmental education in community college. *New Directions for Community Colleges, 145,* 11–30.

39. Buchwitz, B. J., Beyer, C. H., Peterson, J. E., Pitre, E., Lalic, N., Sampson, P. D., & Wakimoto, B. T. (2012). Facilitating long term changes in student approaches to learning science. *CBE–Life Sciences Education, 11*(3), 273–282.

40. Sorby, S. A., & Baartmans, B. J. (2000). The development and assessment of a course for enhancing the 3-D spatial visualization skills of first year engineering students. *Journal of Engineering Education, 89*(3), 301–7.

41. Dweck, C. S. (2006). *Mindset: The new psychology of success.* New York, NY: Random House.

42. Schunk, D. H. (2008). Metacognition, self-regulation, and self-regulated learning: Research recommendations. *Educational Psychology Review, 20*(4), 463–467.

43. Cook, J. E., Purdie-Vaughns, V., Garcia, J., & Cohen, G. L. (2012). Chronic threat and contingent belonging: Protective benefits of values affirmation on identity development. *Journal of Personality and Social Psychology, 102*(3), 479–496.

44. Cohen, G. L., Garcia, J., Purdie-Vaughns, V., Apfel, N., & Brzustoski, P. (2009). Recursive processes in self-affirmation: Intervening to close the minority achievement gap. *Science, 324*(5925), 400–403.

45. Harackiewicz, J. M., Canning, E. A., Tibbetts, Y., Giffen, C. J., Blair, S. S., Rouse, D. I., & Hyde, J. S. (2014). Closing the social class achievement gap for first-generation college students in undergraduate biology. *Journal of Educational Psychology*, 106(2), 375–389.

46. Stout, J. G., & Dasgupta, N. (2011). When he doesn't mean you: Gender-exclusive language as ostracism for women. *Personality and Social Psychology Bulletin, 37*(6), 757–769.

47. Sherman, D. K., Hartson, K. A., Binning, K. R., Purdie-Vaughns, V., Garcia, J., Taborsky-Barba, S., . . . Cohen, G. L. (2013). Deflecting the trajectory and changing the narrative: How self-affirmation affects academic performance and motivation under identity threat. *Journal of Personality and Social Psychology, 104*(4), 591–618. doi:10.1037/a0031495

5

WHAT WORKS (AND WHY) DURING THE TRANSITION TO THE WORKPLACE OR GRADUATE STUDIES

As students consider the transition to the workplace or graduate studies, capacity, interest, and belongingness continue to be crucial factors, primarily in the persistence of students in STEM. Although future careers are in the mind of many students well before they set foot on a college campus or declare a major, the prospect of entering the workplace becomes more salient as students approach graduation. The degree to which departments can support students in developing their capacity to thrive in a STEM profession, as well as their confidence in having that capacity, will make a difference in persistence. Departments may still recruit students and recent graduates who discover STEM late in their college years and only have time to complete a minor or want to return for a second major. How do you help these students pursue a professional opportunity in your field after graduation? Workplace partnerships can help with developing on-ramps into STEM late in college or after graduation.

In this chapter, I focus on capacity to learn. Developing the skills to be successful in the professional realm, whether through internships or professional networking, contributes to persistence. Peer mentors who help newer students in the lab may generate higher order skill development, which is important for continued success in the field.[1] Capstone courses provide a window into what the future career holds. When they include work-related experiences, capstones are even more useful as students strive to develop their professional identity.[2] Capstone courses give students the chance to experiment with a professional identity before deciding whether to pursue graduate studies or accept a position as a STEM professional after graduation.

Interest in STEM also plays a role when students consider whether work in this field will be personally meaningful and align with their other goals. Finally, belongingness is important as students learn about the people who pursue a STEM career, the values in STEM workplaces, and whether they can see themselves in those workplaces or graduate programs. Networking opportunities provide more than connections while students pursue a professional position; they provide images of who the students can be in the future.

The Transition to the Workplace or Graduate Studies: Questions Students Ask

- Do I have the capacity to successfully engage in the professional work in this field?
- Do I know what the work consists of?
- Do I have what it takes to get a job or to get accepted into graduate school?
- Do I know faculty or supervisors well enough to secure strong letters of reference?
- Do I know people in the field and what they do? Would this work be meaningful to me?
- What am I learning in my capstone courses? Are these courses preparing me for a career?
- Do I want to work with the people in my capstone course in the future?
- Do the people I have met through networking opportunities persuade me to join the field?

What Works and Why

In this section I first spotlight four contrasting professional mentoring programs that provide opportunities to develop professional networks and connections. Second, I highlight additional strategies including the design of capstone courses and cooperative workplace partnerships. Third, I address ways to improve departmental climate during the transition to the workplace or graduate studies, focusing on how your department in partnership with employers sends messages to students about what entering the profession will be like.

Spotlight: Four Professional Mentoring Programs

One promising approach to facilitate the transition to the workplace or graduate studies is to offer a professional mentoring program that includes interaction with mentors from various industries. Although networking in the professional sphere should begin earlier than the senior year in college, its relevance does increase as students approach graduation and consider more concretely what will happen after completing their bachelor's degree. Granted, professional networking always has the potential to provide access to opportunities in the workplace, but more than that, the interactions provide valuable insights into the people and practices of the profession and offer a taste of what is to come.[3]

Despite the different focus of professional mentoring programs, they share the following three elements that contribute to their effectiveness:

1. *Professional mentoring programs often involve peer cohorts.* Students who contemplate collectively what awaits after college often feel more at ease during this transition, similar to the way a peer cohort works when students are entering college.[4] Even if a student has concerns about the future profession, being with others who are having similar experiences can be reassuring.
2. *Students benefit from preparation and scaffolding* on professional activities, including internships.[5] Whether you provide instruction on how to use LinkedIn effectively or explain how to request an informational interview, students benefit from explicit instruction.
3. *Professional mentoring programs provide a visible pathway forward* by virtue of their focus on professional connections and role models in the field.[6] Students are motivated by seeing the variety of potential pathways and options to success, so combining work experiences, job shadowing, site visits, and conversations with people in various industries contribute to a more realistic and nuanced view of the working world.

Next, I provide examples of professional mentoring program types. The first example is a formalized program focused on professional mentoring with industry professionals. The second example provides access to networking in STEM organizations' annual meetings, the third example focuses more on building advanced professional experience and a network to create a pipeline to graduate school, and the fourth example focuses on leadership development. In my review of professional mentoring programs, it is rare to find a single program that encompasses all aspects of this transition.

Industry professional mentoring. The largest online professional mentoring program, MentorNet, is designed to connect women and other

underrepresented groups in the sciences to industry professionals (www
.mentornet.net). Originally, colleges and universities paid a fee for access to
MentorNet on their campus, but as of 2011, the program was made available to all college and university students who wish to participate. In 2014,
MentorNet formed a partnership with LinkedIn to advertise mentoring
opportunities to STEM professionals who had indicated an interest in professional volunteering, which widely expanded the pool of potential mentors. The program is considered to be innovative and effective in expanding
the professional networks of college women and people of color who are
considering STEM careers.[7]

MentorNet offers training for students and professionals and then strategically matches students with professionals in pairs for up to four months.[8]
Over the 16 weeks, on average, mentors and students connect via e-mail for
15 minutes per week to discuss that week's scheduled discussion prompt,
which helps the pair address a relevant topic. After a four-month cycle, the
student can request a new mentor, and the prompts are adjusted to fit the
student's academic or career stage. The program's training methods and
implementation have been subjected to rigorous research.[9]

This model can be an excellent complement to a departmental or divi-
sional mentoring program. A group of students in an upper-level course or a
STEM student club could take part in the MentorNet experience together,
or students can participate individually. Some campus administrators prefer to rely on their own alumni because of their stronger connection to the
students at the college, and because the students may more readily imagine
themselves following a similar path.[10] However, you should be prepared to
provide your own in-house training and staff support. You do not want to
involve alumni in a poorly organized program that risks damaging relations
with them. Instead, consider starting conservatively with a one-time event
such as a Skype-based or in-person career panel, an informational interview,
a networking reception, or another type of self-contained event in which the
payoff to both parties will be quickly apparent.

Networking in national organizations. The Society for Chicanos and
Native Americans in Science (SACNAS, see sacnas.org) is a national professional organization that hosts an annual meeting and other activities to
facilitate networking between students and professionals who share these
cultural identities. Professional organizations such as SACNAS and others
(e.g., Society of Women Engineers, Society of Black Engineers, Association
for Women in Science) have a national membership and, as a result, collective resources.[11] Colleges and universities can sponsor a local chapter of these
groups or provide students with access to the national meeting, which leads
to broader networks. If there are few people from a particular demographic

background in your department, this type of group offers these students a more expansive sense of the diversity of the larger professional community. Even if your institution becomes a partner with the organization, students need to find funding to attend the annual meeting, so cost is a major consideration. If you are trying to create a chapter on your own campus, you will want to consider supporting the effort with an on-site coordinator.

Catalyst for graduate school. The University of California's Leadership Excellence Through Advanced Degrees (see www.ucop.edu/graduate-studies/initiatives-outreach/uc-leads.html) is a PhD preparation program targeting underrepresented students in STEM and includes an array of activities such as additional research experience, opportunities to make presentations at national conferences, and networking with universities with strong doctoral programs. The program is similar to other research-focused programs, such as the National Science Foundation's (NSF) Research Experience for Undergraduates (www.nsf.gov/crssprgm/reu), in that it specifically emphasizes the importance of pursuing a doctorate. While such programs are effective, not all students want to pursue a doctoral program or enter the professoriate.

Leadership development. Many upper-level students benefit from leadership development opportunities, such as the previously mentioned multiyear research experiences and the chance to serve as a supplemental instructor or FSG leader. The STARS Computing Corps (www.starscomputingcorps .org) program, in which industry partners can participate, forms a leadership cohort that provides outreach activities that target newer students in computing. Alternatively, some campuses offer a fellowship or scholars group for teaching assistants, while others may have honor societies or other ways to develop leadership. The positive outcome of this program is that students gain a stronger connection to the field by serving in a leadership position and taking on the responsibility of providing outreach or teaching others.[12] However, the experience of providing outreach or educational support by itself may not be enough to ensure a successful transition into the profession.

Initiative Highlights

Although a professional mentoring program can help support students in the out-of-college transition, the approach does not meet all the needs of the students. In this section, I review the design of capstone courses and the design of workplace partnerships, both of which are especially important for providing on-ramps for students who discover STEM later in college.

Capstone course design: Team- and community-based learning. Many departments already have capstone courses that provide opportunities for students to integrate what they have previously learned as well as take on challenging new material. For example, students often have a chance to design or build a project, conduct research, or run a program. In a capstone project, students develop solutions to ill-structured problems, receive guidance and feedback from the instructor, and work actively with group members.[13] Capstone projects are also often interdisciplinary in nature, incorporating new understanding and applications.[14]

A major benefit of capstone courses is that students often work in a team, providing a cohort experience among majors on the cusp of graduation. Capstones provide opportunities for departments to provide group-level advising, including preparing for the job search, learning how to form a relationship with people in a future workplace, or improving applications to graduate school.

Most capstones integrate reflective and goal-setting exercises. Two practices frequently employed in capstone courses are team-based learning practices and community-based projects. Here, I review key research explaining how these approaches can be implemented effectively.

Not all instructors of capstone projects who use project-based learning, in which students work in small teams, also truly utilize team-based learning, even if they break the class into project groups. Team-based learning takes group work to a new level. Most often used in health professions and business courses, but now increasingly used in other disciplines, the team-based learning approach relies on certain principles that recognize the team as a learning entity separate from the individual.[15] In team-based learning, grades are given to individuals and to the team; the team develops knowledge, team members rate each other, and they produce a collective product. The idea is that students are gaining experience with practices they will likely encounter in the workplace. In addition, there is evidence that students learn more collectively than they can alone.[16] Still another benefit is that being connected to a small team can be motivating.[17]

While there is no set maximum group size, many studies agree on groups of no more than six people to avoid situations in which students take advantage of the others or rely on the efforts of others.[18] In smaller groups individual participants are more apt to feel accountable and make a contribution.

Team composition is a key element in team-based learning. Participants should be randomly selected and diverse in terms of race, gender, and other characteristics. Research suggests that engineering teams deliberately formed to include at least 75% of women are more likely to foster active participation from the women than groups that are 50% or 25% women.[19] The literature on this powerful pedagogy offers considerable guidance on team formation because team members work closely together and are graded as a group, so they have to develop trust. Other guidance from the literature includes how to structure problems and scaffold the knowledge students need to develop solutions. Capstones using team-based learning offer an opportunity for instructors to provide explicit teaching about working in a team that can benefit all students as they head into the workplace or graduate school.

That being said, is important to note that faculty who use these pedagogies should do so only after careful preparation and with a full understanding of the advantages and the downsides. You may find it beneficial to create a faculty learning community for the faculty teaching a capstone course so they can provide support to one another and share ideas.[20] While not necessary for team-based learning, it can also be advantageous to have access to so-called *smart classrooms* with an open floor plan, round tables, and computer stations and projection capability.

Community-based learning initiatives are powerful and considered a high-impact practice that promotes engagement and persistence.[21] Thus, it should come as no surprise that capstone courses often include a community-based project and that students find these experiences to be transformative. Reciprocity is a key component of community engagement, meaning that the project is of mutual benefit to the students and the community partner. The community partner sets the agenda, while students contribute their knowledge base and subject expertise in the service of a community organization or business. In one capstone course, students enlisted as trainee programmers in a community organization where they cocreated action plans that contributed to the organization as well as deepened their own learning.[22] The University of Nebraska–Lincoln used an approach called Math in the City in one of its capstone courses in which students worked with various partners including a medical center where they identified risk factors in heart disease and an architecture firm where they examined sustainable design.[23] At Oakland University, administrators and faculty designed multidisciplinary capstone courses to develop a toy or game prototype for an organization, increasing students' motivation by working with a real-world audience.[24] Partnerships require close coordination of goals and a clear understanding of the roles and resources each party brings to the table.[25] Talking to faculty in other departments who have completed such capstone projects or contacting your campus center for community engagement or service-learning would be a good starting point in developing this kind of project.

In the next section I discuss partnerships with workplaces. Cooperative work experiences and community-based projects are not mutually exclusive categories. Indeed, many capstone courses can be arranged to integrate real-world experiences with a community partner that allows the students to work in the organization. I make the distinction between community-based projects and cooperative work experiences because in many cases cooperative work experiences may be used outside the context of a capstone course.

Workplace partnerships: Leveraging cooperative work and creating on-ramps.
Department administrators need to actively create workplace partnerships,
and not just for internships. Workplace partnerships can provide on-ramps
for students who discover STEM late in college or after they complete their
degree. Having a range of strong workplace partners also helps fuel your
department's alumni network and keeps you in close contact with the norms
and expectations in an industry.

Some colleges and universities establish a co-op program with nearby
workplaces for course credit or for paid internships. Engineering program
directors frequently use this model, which allows students to earn credit or
receive a salary in a workplace as part of the major (e.g., see Northwestern's
engineering program, www.mccormick.northwestern.edu). The Urban Massachusetts Louis Stokes Alliance for Minority Participation, funded by NSF
and involving several higher education institutions including community
colleges and four-year universities in Massachusetts, gives students the opportunity to work as interns in an academic information technology department or in a research lab, assisting staff and gaining relevant work experience
(see www.uml.edu/docs/UMLSAMP%20Brochure_tcm18-108242.pdf).
These work experiences help students clarify their career directions as well
as provide the requisite experience needed to gain entry to postbaccalaureate
employment or graduate school.[26]

There are some drawbacks to this approach; unlike capstone courses,
cooperative work experiences may be a solo experience, and students may not
have opportunities to process what they observe or experience in the workplace. The quality of the on-site work supervisor matters, too, and vetting
employer partners and ongoing monitoring by the department has its costs.
In addition, if a student participates in only one rotation in one workplace,
that single experience may be the student's only example of what working
in the field is like, whether positive or negative. Departments might explore
alternative initiatives that provide job shadowing or site visits to various
workplaces to supplement a cooperative work experience. In some majors,
cooperative work experiences that take place during the academic year may
not be feasible. In this case, summer internships may make more sense but
may raise questions about how to create cohort experiences among interns in
your department and how to help students make sense of what they learned.
In some cases, students will find out they are on the wrong career path; in
other cases, without a trusted adviser, students are unable to process what
they learned, which might lead some students to turn away from the field
without further exploration.[27]

Beyond internships, ongoing relationships with workplaces are beneficial for departments and recent alumni. Students who discover STEM later
in their academic careers cannot always see how pursuing it can be a feasible

option. For example, transfer students who know they want to pursue STEM but end up taking a range of introductory courses in biology, chemistry, and geology might be able to cobble together a minor in STEM but not necessarily a major. Other students might discover computer science when taking a course in their senior year and want to a find a way to continue their learning and translate that learning into a career.

One idea is to create a flexible STEM minor that allows students to highlight their résumé and transcript with a STEM-oriented program of study and help them to find a related internship or cocurricular experience. If a minor is not possible, students can be encouraged to take a course or two to gain relevant skills (e.g., coding, field research, or statistics) before undertaking a postbaccalaureate path.

Another idea is for departments to create a postbaccalaureate program or a fast-track master's program targeting individuals who are non-STEM majors but have taken some of the key prerequisites. Although they are more frequently used for medical school and teacher licensure preparation, postbaccalaureate approaches could be promising for STEM fields. Many business, education, and policy-oriented graduate programs currently target STEM students. It would behoove administrators of STEM departments to consider encouraging non-STEM students to take a second look at STEM after graduation.

Still another on-ramp for students are weekend or low-residency programs that incorporate some degree of distance education. These programs can help employed individuals build their credentials or create access for those returning for a second bachelor's degree, particularly in technical fields. Such innovative programs send the message that it is not too late to pursue a career in STEM.

Transition to the Workplace or Graduate Studies: Reader Questions

- How do majors experience your capstone courses?
- Is there a mechanism that allows students to merge into the major through a postbaccalaureate program? Do you offer a flexible minor?
- Do you have workplace partnerships, not just for internships but also for recent graduates to think about developing their skill set through a second bachelor's or graduate degree?

Improving Departmental Climate for Upper-Level Students

Students' experiences during the transition into the workplace or graduate studies are influenced by the learning environment, in particular in capstone courses, as well as through their work experiences. Climate is also influenced by your department's provision of resources to support the professional development of faculty to implement new pedagogies, revamp capstone courses, and support student access to internships in the workplace. Bear in mind that students are looking closely at the implicit messages communicated by academic and industry workplaces, which influence whether they can envision themselves moving toward a career in those areas. Workplace environments provide clues about their commitment to diversity through the people who work there, their philosophies, and norms.[28] Students shift their mind-set into that of prospective employees, and they pay attention to the following characteristics.

Critical mass (versus token status). Students examine how their demographic identities are represented in various workplaces. Will they become tokens, one or two here or there, or will they achieve critical mass? Critical mass sends members of underrepresented groups a message of identity safety and that valuation.[29]

Diversity philosophy (versus color blind). Students search for the department's philosophy on diversity and the philosophy of other employers as an indicator of inclusiveness in the work environment. In the absence of such a philosophy, students will infer that there is none or that the prevailing philosophy is color blind. At one time, being color blind translated to acceptance (i.e., everyone is the same); however, today it is believed that this approach denies difference and erases the cultural assets and perspectives of people of color. An employer's diversity statement sends a message of inclusion to underrepresented prospective employees and to all employees searching for a workplace that values people from a range of backgrounds and perspectives.[30] Of course the statement should be accompanied by real and visible action.

Variability of identity (versus stereotypical images). Students examine which identities are valued in the workplace. For example, if only *science*

Departmental Climate Ideas: Upper-Level Students

- Consider which workplaces you showcase, and why. Do particular workplaces have exemplary diversity philosophies? Is there a critical mass for particular groups of students?
- Consider your own departmental climate in regard to civility and hostility. What do students observe about the profession through the way you demonstrate it?
- Consider what your classrooms, hallways, and study spaces communicate about the energy of your department.

fiction or male-oriented posters or other indicators of STEM stereotypes are present, this tells a new student or employee that he or she must fit into a particular mold to work there.[31]

Workplace civility (versus hostility). Students pay attention to interactions among colleagues at work. Hostile exchanges have a negative impact on not only the recipient of but also those watching such exchanges, to the detriment of the workplace as a whole.[32]

Case Study: Mark Sanderson

In this section I illustrate the process of designing mentoring initiatives during the transition to the workplace or graduate studies using the case of Mark Sanderson, this book's focal STEM dean, who works at a university branch campus. He wants to improve the experiences of transfer students who are mostly first-generation college students. They are struggling in the job search process, and he wants to build an initiative that addresses their needs.

Step 1: Understand the Factors

Mark has identified first-generation college students, many of whom are transfers from community college, as his target. Based on a first look at his enrollment data, he decides to focus on engineering students because they make up a sizable number of the students who transfer. He asks himself the following:

- How do first-generation or college transfer students fare on the job market as compared to their peers?
- Why do they struggle with the job search?

To find out more, Mark draws from a range of sources. He consults with the admissions department to determine the top feeder schools for community college transfer students. Few students consider a transfer-based program in engineering because they do not anticipate being able to complete the program in the time that they are eligible to receive financial aid (usually four to five semesters).

Let's say he finds out that 500 majors graduate with engineering degrees at his institution each year; roughly 175 of them are transfers, and about 60% of those are first-generation. Let's also say that his institutional data show that 70% of the transfers land jobs in engineering after graduation, but only one in three of those were first-generation college students.

To find out more about his students' job search experiences, he consults the six-month postgraduation alumni survey from the university.

TABLE 5.1
Mark's Primary Obstacles and Mentoring Goals

Mark's Primary Obstacles	Mark's Mentoring Goals
Students do not have support in the job search, such as interview preparation.	Integrate job search preparation into their experience, possibly through the capstone course.
Some students know little about potential workplaces.	Integrate exposure to and information about various employers.
Students feel isolated in the capstone course.	Integrate stronger team-based learning elements and job search strategies.

Respondents had positive comments about the learning in their capstone course, which provided a rigorous design project, but they still felt isolated in their learning during the course. They cited the challenges of not having a network in the professional field after graduation and the absence of support in their job search. As a result, they reported feeling unprepared in their job interviews. The career center did not appear to facilitate access to a range of workplaces, and a few of the survey respondents worried about their possible fit in the workplace. As a result, they considered going to graduate school in a completely different field or pursuing a different line of work after graduation (see Table 5.1). While these obstacles were shared by all alumni, the barriers appeared to disproportionately affect first-generation college graduates.

Step 2: Choose a Mentoring Strategy

Mark wants to take advantage of professional mentoring resources. He is interested in trying MentorNet, and he will also consult members of the local Society for Women Engineers chapter to learn more about what they might be able to offer his students. He plans to form a partnership with the alumni association and the career development center to explore a collaborative approach to working with alumni. In any effort involving alumni, Mark wants to include recent graduates who were transfer students. He needs to find a service provider to help students learn how to network, interview for a position, and meet an array of industry professionals. Ideally his efforts would be integrated into the existing capstone course, possibly by adding a new lab component or a fourth hour to the course. Finally, he will try to intensify the team-based learning component. In general, his department administrators should think about their workplace partnerships, including the cultures of different workplaces and how to present an array of choices to students.

TABLE 5.2
Mark's Mentoring Strategy and Plan

Mentoring Goals (Outcomes You Hope For)	Activities to Facilitate Mentoring (Programs, Practices, Events)	What Resources Are Needed? (Existing Programs? External Grants?)	How Will You Know If the Initiative Is Successful?
Fit in field	Professional mentoring via MentorNet	Sign-up costs	Reports in exit year focus groups
Belongingness in capstone	Team-based project	Access to capstone instructors and their interest in doing this	Course evaluations
Knowledge of workplaces/ interest	Guest visitors, possibly alumni	Form partnership with the career center or alumni association	Reports by students after sessions
Capability in: job search	Capstone course	Access to lab or add a fourth hour, partnership with career center or alumni	Evaluations, one-year-out surveys, job placements

Step 3: Does This Plan Make Sense?

Mark's initial resource inventory is promising. He already has a well-functioning capstone course, but he needs to add new components (see Table 5.2).

Mark's logic model includes targeting the student-to-professional transition through a combination of strategies. He hopes to find a way to infuse professional mentoring opportunities into capstone courses by creating access to professional mentors (possibly alumni), site visits, and job search and interview support. Mark's if/then statement is the following:

> If I change the experience in the engineering capstone course to include more exposure to career possibilities, workplaces, and professionals, and support in the preparation for the job search and interview, then I will see more students, including more transfer students who are first-generation, find jobs or be accepted to graduate school in engineering.

Step 4: Start Small With a Pilot, and Track Progress

Mark can start small by adding more preparation for employment interviews into the course as well as team-based learning and visits to different workplaces, which could be costly if they are not nearby.

Reader Next Steps: Explore Your Options During the Transition to the Workplace or Graduate Studies

Which models do you already have in your department? Which ones do you want to explore?

Transition Options

Initiative Type	We Have This	I Want to Explore This
Summer research		
Internships		
Capstone courses		
Job preparation workshops		
Team-based learning		
Community-based projects		
Professional mentoring programs		
Guests in classes		
Other ideas:		

Your Goals, Activities, Resources, and Indicators

Mentoring Goals (Outcomes You Hope For)	Activities to Facilitate Mentoring (Programs, Practices, Events)	What Resources Are Needed? (Existing Programs? External Grants?)	How Will You Know If the Initiative Is Successful? (Indicators of Progress)

Your If/Then Statements

If I _____ ,

then _____ .

If _____ ,

then _____ .

Pilot: What would a pilot look like for your initiative(s)?

Tracking: How will you know when your initiative has been successful?

Notes

1. Thiry, H., Weston, T. J., Laursen, S. L., & Hunter, A. (2012). The benefits of multi-year research experiences: Differences in novice and experienced students' reported gains from undergraduate research. *CBE–Life Sciences Education, 11*(3), 260–272.

2. Trede, F. (2012). Role of work-integrated learning in developing professionalism and professional identity. *Asia-Pacific Journal of Cooperative Education, 13*(3), 159–167.

3. Ibarra, H. (1999). Provisional selves: Experimenting with image and identity in professional adaptation. *Administrative Science Quarterly, 44*(4), 764–791.

4. Park, G., Spitzmuller, M., & DeShon, R. P. (2013). Advancing our understanding of team motivation: Integrating conceptual approaches and content areas. *Journal of Management, 39*(5), 1339–1379.

5. Charney, J., Hmelo-Silver, C. E., Sofer, W., Neigeborn, L., Coletta, S., & Nemeroff, M. (2007). Cognitive apprenticeship in science through immersion in laboratory practices. *International Journal of Science Education, 29*(2), 195–213.

6. Ibarra, H. (1999). Provisional selves: Experimenting with image and identity in professional adaptation. *Administrative Science Quarterly, 44*(4), 764–791.

7. Barker, L., & McGrath Cohoon, J. (2015). *What makes electronic mentoring effective? MentorNet—www.MentorNet.com (Case study 1).* Retrieved from National Center for Women & Information Technology website: www.ncwit.org/resources/what-makes-electronic-mentoring-effective-mentornet-wwwmentornetnet-case-study-1

8. Blake-Beard, S., Bayne, M. L., Crosby, F. J., & Muller, C. B. (2011). Matching by race and gender in mentoring relationships: Keeping our eyes on the prize. *Journal of Social Issues, 67*(3), 622–643.

9. Kasprisin, C. A., Boyle Single, P., Single, R. M., & Muller, C. B. (2003). Building a better bridge: Testing e-training to improve e-mentoring programs for diversity in higher education. *Mentoring & Tutoring: Partnerships in Learning, 11*(1), 67–78.

10. Packard, B. W., & Hudgings, J. H. (2002). Expanding college women's perceptions of physicists' lives and work through interactions with a physics careers web site. *Journal of College Science Teaching, 32*(3), 164–170.

11. Chemers, M. M., Zurbriggen, E. L., Syed, M., Goza, B. K., & Bearman, S. (2011). The role of efficacy and identity in science career commitment among underrepresented minority students. *Journal of Social Issues, 67*(3), 469–491. doi:10.1111/j.1540-4560.2011.01710.x

12. Marquez Kiyama, J., & Guillen Luca, S. (2013–2014). Structured opportunities: Exploring the social and academic benefits for peer mentors in retention programs. *Journal of College Student Retention, 15*(4), 489–514.

13. Jones, B. D., Epler, C. M., Mokri, P., Bryant, L. H., & Paretti, M. C. (2013). The effects of a collaborative problem-based learning experience on students' motivation in engineering capstone courses. *Interdisciplinary Journal of Problem-Based Learning, 7*(2), 34–71.

14. Weyhaupt, A. G. (2013). A real-life data project for an interdisciplinary math and politics course. *PRIMUS, 23*(1), 13–24.

15. Michaelsen, L. K., & Sweet, M. (2008). The essential elements of team-based learning. *New Directions for Teaching & Learning*, 116, 7–27.

16. Michaelsen, L. K., & Sweet, M. (2008). The essential elements of team-based learning. *New Directions for Teaching & Learning*, 116, 7–27.

17. Park, G., Spitzmuller, M., & DeShon, R. P. (2013). Advancing our understanding of team motivation: Integrating conceptual approaches and content areas. *Journal of Management, 39*(5), 1339–1379.

18. Griffin, P. M., Griffin, S. O., Llewellyn, D. C. (2004). The impact of group size and project duration on capstone design. *Journal of Engineering Education, 93*(3), 185–193.

19. Dasgupta, N., McManus Scircle, M., & Hunsinger, M. (2015). *Female peers in small work groups enhance women's motivation, verbal participation, and career aspirations in engineering.* Retrieved from www.pnas.org/content/early/2015/04/03/1422822112

20. Moore, J. A., & Carter-Hicks, J. (2014). Let's talk! Facilitating a faculty learning community using a critical friends group approach. *International Journal for the Scholarship of Teaching & Learning, 8*(2), 1–17.

21. Kuh, G. D., & Schneider, C. G. (2008). *High-impact educational practices: What they are, who has access to them, and why they matter.* Washington, DC: Association of American Colleges and Universities.

22. Chang, Y., Wang, T., Chen, S., & Liao, R. (2011). Student engineers as agents of change: Combining social inclusion in the professional development of electrical and computer engineering students. *Systemic Practice and Action Research, 24*(3), 237–245.

23. Radu, P. (2013). Taking math outside of the classroom: Math in the city. *PRIMUS, 23*(6), 538–549.

24. Latcha, M., & Oakley, B. (2001). Toying with a capstone design course. *Journal of Engineering Education, 90*(4), 627–629.

25. Maloni, M. J., & Paul, R. C. (2011). A service learning campus sustainability project. *Decision Sciences Journal of Innovative Education, 9*(1), 101–106.

26. Hart Research and Associates. (2013). *It takes more than a major: Employer priorities for college learning and student success.* Retrieved from www.aacu.org/sites/default/files/files/LEAP/2013_EmployerSurvey.pdf

27. Packard, B. W., & Nguyen, D. (2003). Science career-related possible selves of adolescent girls: A longitudinal study. *Journal of Career Development, 29*(4), 251–263.

28. Emerson, K. T. U., & Murphy, M. C. (2014). Identity threat at work: How social identity threat and situational cues contribute to racial and ethnic disparities in the workplace. *Cultural Diversity and Ethnic Minority Psychology, 20*(4), 508–520.

29. Murphy, M. C., Steele, C. M., & Gross, J. J. (2007). Signaling threat: How situational cues affect women in math, science, and engineering settings. *Psychological Science, 18*(10), 879–885.

30. Purdie-Vaughns, V., Steele, C. M., Davies, P. G., Ditlmann, R., & Crosby, J. R. (2008). Social identity contingencies: How diversity cues signal threat or safety for African Americans in mainstream institutions. *Journal of Personality and Social Psychology, 94*(4), 615–630. doi:10.1037/0022-3514.94.4.615

31. Cheryan, S., Plaut, V. C., Davies, P. G., & Steele, C. M. (2009). Ambient belonging: How stereotypical cues impact gender participation in computer science. *Journal of Personality and Social Psychology, 97*(6), 1045–1060. doi:10.1037/a0016239

32. Miner-Rubino, K., & Cortina, L. M. (2007). Beyond targets: Consequences of vicarious exposure to misogyny at work. *Journal of Applied Psychology, 92*(5), 1254–1269. doi:10.1037/0021-9010.92.5.1254

6

DIFFICULT MENTORING MOMENTS
Framing Messages to Improve Impact

In this chapter I turn to the nuances that influence the effectiveness of mentoring initiatives. Despite good intentions and planning, the power of mentoring is not always realized because mentoring is based on interactions among people, whether in formal programs, classrooms, advising spaces, research labs, hallways, or events. I hope the content of this chapter will make your mentoring messages and initiatives more effective. Let me remind you: One student, one colleague, one interaction at a time.

Because this book is written for faculty and administrators, I focus on some difficult mentoring messages from the vantage point of the mentor. I analyze four common mentoring interactions whose messages can be challenging to frame effectively and provide recommendations on how each message can be reframed to improve communication and increase the likelihood that the student will hear or act on the message. I'm not suggesting you memorize a set of scripts, although I do provide some sample language. By understanding the impact of how we frame messages, we can work toward finding authentic ways to communicate effectively.

Why Some Mentoring Moments Are Difficult

Although we may wish that all mentoring interactions could focus on the positive, the reality is that mentoring also involves difficulty. Interpersonal communication can be challenging to get right because what the mentor intends to say is not always what the student hears, whether the mentor is trying to inspire a student or provide critical feedback. It is even more difficult to try to recover from a misstep or awkward exchange with a student that is unsettling to both parties.

Much of the mentoring discussed in this book aims to facilitate interactions among people from different backgrounds (e.g., White male faculty mentors working with women or people of color who are first-generation college students). Since we live and work in a world with structural inequities and negative stereotypes about underrepresented groups, the possibility for misunderstanding can intensify when people communicate across race, gender, socioeconomic status, or other social identities. Because people vary in their lived experiences, their perspectives vary too, which may affect how they hear certain kinds of comments. Indeed, what is heard is often influenced by who is talking and how messages are framed.[1]

In cross-race, cross-gender, cross-class, and other cross-identity communications, the possibility for miscommunication is high because the *intent* or reason for providing the feedback may not be understood by the recipients when they are members of a stigmatized group. A student may wonder whether the speaker doesn't believe in the student because of the student's racial, gender, or class identity, or because the quality of the work itself is bad. Miscommunication can occur however well-intentioned the speaker is because bias is so prevalent in our society.[2] That being said, good mentoring makes it possible to develop trust and improve communication with underrepresented students.[3]

Some faculty, staff, or peer mentors try to avoid difficult interactions, particularly when it comes to feedback, because they are worried about the possibility of saying the wrong thing or for fear of appearing racist or gender biased. For example, researchers found that White clinical supervisors may hesitate to provide Black graduate students with critical performance feedback.[4] In another study, advisers assigned to Black college students were more likely to withhold warnings about a possible course overload for fear of appearing racist.[5] In yet another study, researchers reported that faculty sometimes chose to gloss over the student's performance.[6] Avoiding a tough conversation only serves to postpone disappointment for the student because weaknesses in performance or future academic plans are likely to be exposed at a later time. Although it may be difficult to do, providing that critical but constructive feedback is important to help students grow.

Here, I discuss four common messages that mentors may send when giving feedback to students: giving critical feedback on a student's performance or plans without being discouraging, avoiding inspirational messages that inadvertently undermine a student's motivation, redirecting a student's request without the student feeling brushed off, and recovering from a misstep or microaggression. The goal of feedback is to motivate the student to engage in deeper reflection and action, and to position you (or the mentors in your initiatives) as capable, appreciated, and effective.

Message 1: "You Don't Have What It Takes."

We regularly offer students critical feedback about their performance or proposed plans, such as for course schedules or applications for graduate school. We cannot watch students participate in a faulty research process or complete academic work incorrectly and just let it go without a conversation. Equally, if a student proposes a plan of study that is destined for failure, we should not endorse that plan. To truly invest in students, mentors should create opportunities for students to benefit from the mentor's candid assessment of their work or plans. When mentoring is viewed as a developmental relationship, the goal is to help students grow from constructive feedback. *Constructive* is the key word. How do you communicate the need for improvement in a way that is not devastating? While we rarely want to say to students, "You don't have what it takes," they may construe a critique as conveying this negative message and lose all motivation to improve, even if they have the potential and the interest.

It is important to be as candid as possible about poor-quality work and avoid sugarcoating feedback. If you recognize that a student's work is inadequate, your job as a mentor is to help the student obtain the confidence, tools, and advice necessary to improve. Explain that you are confident in the student's capability to meet a higher standard and that you are providing the feedback because you take the student seriously and know the student's goals are important to him or her.[7] When you explain the reason for the feedback—that you are taking the student seriously—the student is more apt to tune in to what you are saying. Also, by leading with this statement of confidence in the student, you can at least in part neutralize the mistrust triggered by introducing critical feedback. Instead of just leading with a positive comment to soften the blow of the forthcoming negative comment, you need to frame the feedback in a way that can help the student grow as you make your recommendations for the student to try new actions or strategies. In doing so, your message reinforces the growth mind-set in which ability is viewed as incremental rather than fixed, and this is empowering for the student.[8]

Similarly, when a student presents a plan that poses problems, such as applying for an internship without the appropriate qualifications or including materials that were poorly proofread (and wants you to provide a letter of reference), you can begin by stating that you believe in the student and recognize how invested the student is in the plan, but there are drawbacks and you want to be able to point them out. In certain situations you can depersonalize critical feedback and increase the likelihood the student will respond to it by giving your advice proactively in a group setting without identifying any individuals, and even before any of the typical reasons for providing critical feedback have surfaced. Many department administrators and advisers know the kinds of proposals students are considering such as their course schedules, possible internships, and applications to graduate schools. Communicating to students as a group can help dispel any idea that some of them are receiving certain messages while others are not. In addition, citing an authority, such as employers, alumni, or graduate school staff, can add credibility to your message and remove the perception that it's a personal opinion.[9] For example, when a student is applying to graduate school you can suggest that the student request an informational interview with two alumni to gain more insight into the process.

You won't always feel comfortable saying you have high expectations for each and every student. But the reality is, you don't know who will rise to the challenge. We can all think of examples where a student has surprised us. The framing I recommend will help the student feel the feedback was fair, informative, and encouraging. By separating the work or the plan from

---

Offering Critical Feedback About Poor Performance or Plans

- This work has not met the mark. This plan has drawbacks we should discuss.
- This process is difficult for many people.
- I have high standards as do graduate schools or employers.
- I know you can meet this high standard. You are capable of better work.
- I am going to give you this feedback because I take you seriously.
- Are you willing to try some different strategies?
- I'm willing to help you discuss the results after you try new strategies and see what works.
- The top-rated graduate schools recommend two years of lab experience.
- It's helpful to you to seek expert advice. You could contact a few graduate schools, alumni, or employers. Here is an interview template from the career center.
- We could discuss what you learn after you talk to more people.
- Let's develop a plan that will give you the best chance of reaching your goal.[10]

the person, and by suggesting resources for the student to seek additional information, the student is likely to come to an informed conclusion. Ultimately, when a student hears that you take his or her plans seriously enough to provide candid feedback, that student is more likely to be motivated and regard you as helpful. Practice framing constructive feedback that feels authentic to you.

Message 2: "I'm Amazing. Be Like Me."

Even inspirational messages may be tough to craft effectively. We may craft a message intending to inspire students but end up deflating their motivation instead.[11] Just think about how many events you have walked out of thinking that the speaker missed the mark with the audience.

Asking guests to speak about their lives is flattering, and it is natural that many focus on their successes and how amazing they are. Unfortunately, by emphasizing one's perfections, speakers decrease the power of their message because the message is not in sync with what the students are hearing.[12] Whatever the speaker's intention, the student will hear, "I'm amazing. Be like me," and the student may think, "I'm not as smart or talented as that person. I'm not like that person; that message does not apply to me." Students listen to find how the message is relevant to them and to their pathways. You want to help speakers craft compelling messages worth listening to.

How do you create resonance and relevance in a message? First, search for speakers who are just a step ahead of your students or who can readily connect to students. Superstars in a field have name recognition, which is an asset, but they may also need to be reminded to adapt their story so that it is relevant to the student in the audience. Stars on the rise, who are closer to the students' professional stage, should not be overlooked because students can more readily imagine themselves taking the same next steps. Short-term goals can enhance motivation as students move toward their long-term goals.[13]

Second, speakers engage listeners when they emphasize the struggles they overcame before they achieved success. When speakers say they always knew what they wanted to do or were always good at everything, students struggle to see similarities; in contrast, speakers who emphasize the struggle before success are generally more inspirational for students.[14] In a research study, new students were more motivated to persist when they heard a panel of upper-level students talk about the struggles and opportunities they faced as first-generation college students than when they heard speakers who said they were first-generation college students but provided no information on the challenges they faced or opportunities they had relating to their social identity.[15] Alumni role models are especially motivating and relevant.[16]

Third, relevance can be enhanced by inviting multiple people to speak, as they offer more potential connection points with students and a greater variety of experiences.[17] If you are constructing a panel, consider ways to provide students with different, nonstereotypical perspectives.[18] If you are hosting only one speaker or one mentor, ask the speaker to encourage students to learn about additional pathways and strategies or contrast the speaker's own trajectory with other powerful examples when possible.[19]

These strategies are also suitable for one-on-one student advising. You can share coping messages on topics such as overcoming a major challenge, refer students to additional resources, or talk about the experiences of past students. It's important to craft messages that combine inspiration with reality to help students see the relevance to their lives.

Crafting Inspirational, Relevant Messages

- I want to tell you my pathway. I was asked to speak to you because of my successes.
- I also want to tell you about an obstacle I overcame.
- You might be thinking we are not alike, or what I tried would not work for you.
- Here is what is similar about us.
- This is why something like this could work for you.
- My pathway is just one pathway. There are many pathways to get where you want to go.
- One action you can take next is to improve your skill in (writing, public speaking, statistics, etc.).
- Keep going by taking actions that take you a step closer to your goal.
- If you are not sure what that next step is for you, talk to someone about it.
- Choose someone who knows this is your goal and will help you reach that goal.
- Keep working toward your goals.[20]

Message 3: "No, I Can't Help You."

This example gets at the heart of how small interactions can add up to make a big difference. For example, a student may come to you with a particular set of questions, and you know someone else has more expertise. How do you refer students to other advisers or resources without giving the impression that you're brushing them off?

Many students seek advice through an array of channels. Although we often have to advise students to seek expert advice from others, students sometimes return feeling alienated or that they have hit a dead end.[21] As a representative of your field of study, you want the student to know you are trying to be helpful, and that the people in your department are approachable and available to answer questions.

My advice here is simple: Provide a helpful suggestion for a next step. For example, you can suggest an alternative resource to pursue. Students often appreciate advice that helps them better understand how to formulate their question or identify someone to help them. If you give them this kind of direction, you will be perceived as resourceful, and the student will feel supported as well as motivated to pursue the next step.[22] I'm not saying students should not learn how to handle rejection; they must learn to face challenges and overcome them. I am saying it can be good for STEM faculty and administrators to offer helpful suggestions. Being resourceful can provide students with a positive sense of the department, and students may be more likely to leave feeling supported, even though they were redirected by someone in that department.

Referring a Student Elsewhere

I am unable to help you because (state the reason), however,

- I know your goal is important to you, and I want to steer you in the right direction.
- Let me help you work on the next step or determine to where you can turn.
- I could introduce you to (an expert), or I can give you (the person's) contact information.
- Don't be discouraged by having to pursue multiple leads; this is part of the process.[23]

Message 4: "[Silence.] I Hope You Didn't Notice That."

Sometimes we inadvertently make comments that may be offensive because of the student's race, gender, or another social identity. Some STEM faculty or administrators have a false sense of security because they think they are insulated from making personal comments because their teaching centers on polymers or plant biology, rather than human beings. In the classroom, the lab, or in an informal conversation, race, class, or gender can come up unexpectedly, or students could feel slighted or excluded in group work because of their social identity. Indeed, even during your own office hours and in the lab you may find yourself making comments unconsciously that are offensive or reveal a bias.

Microaggressions are defined as "subtle, innocuous, preconscious, or unconscious degradations, and putdowns" that accumulate over time and contribute to negative outcomes including stress and withdrawal from participating.[24] These interpersonal slights often occur during everyday exchanges, and they need not be intentional in order to cause harm.[25] Different types of microaggressions include: microassaults, which many of us recognize as overt racist comments, derogatory racial slurs, or exclusionary language ("Our group is full, go find another group"); microinsults, which are insensitive comments that degrade the intellect or value of a particular group (e.g., "You are the smartest Black/female student I have ever met!" "You don't seem Mexican"); and microinvalidations, which minimize or disregard the feelings of underrepresented students ("I'm sure that's not what she meant, no one is biased here"). Overall, microaggressions function to communicate lowered expectations or to exclude students who come away from the exchange feeling marginalized and excluded, outsiders on their own campus.[26]

Although quite visible and hurtful to the recipient, microaggressions are often invisible to the initiator, who consequently is unlikely to take action, let alone apologize.[27] Because microinsults and microinvalidations are subtle, recipients expend mental and emotional energy replaying interactions to decipher the intention of messages.[28] Particularly in predominantly White college environments, a repetitive cycle of insults, time-consuming interpretation, and dejection can contribute to a sense of battle fatigue among underrepresented students.[29] Similar experiences are also reported by faculty of color, including slights from colleagues about their accomplishments or being challenged in their own classrooms by their students.[30] Teaching assistants of color and from international backgrounds also report microaggressions by faculty and supervising teachers, leading to self-doubt and a fear of entering a profession.[31]

Those least likely to experience microaggressions are also most likely to express skepticism and think their underrepresented peers are oversensitive or paranoid.[32] Being a member of a privileged group (e.g., White, male, able-bodied, etc.) limits the ability to see the reach of one's own privilege, leading to unawareness of the daily discrimination faced by underrepresented individuals.[33] Unfortunately, when White faculty or colleagues (or others) cast underrepresented students or staff as oversensitive and minimize the effect of their negative cumulative experiences, they contribute negatively to the overall climate experienced by underrepresented groups.[34]

The important message here is that there are ways to remedy and recover from difficult exchanges that arise from microaggressions. For guidance, there is a growing body of research literature focused on *difficult dialogues*, defined as discussions on the examination of privilege, racism, legitimacy, or other topics that are likely to elicit discomfort, stress, or defensive reactions.[35] When faced with a microaggression, or another form of bias, exclusion, or putdown, many faculty will choose to remain uncomfortably silent, try to divert attention, or squash discussion about the exchange. Unfortunately, these strategies, although tempting, do not alleviate tension and are viewed negatively by students.[36] Underrepresented students and many majority students leave classes feeling negative about the class, their peers, or the faculty member when microaggressions or problematic dynamics that have occurred are not addressed.[37]

The fear some White individuals have about opening a can of worms over a hot topic (e.g., race) is natural and common if they do not believe they can effectively handle the aftermath.[38] Remember, your students will be watching to see how you (or the mentors in an initiative you design) handle the situation, and what they observe is an important indicator of your trust-worthiness and commitment to inclusion as well as what working in this field will be like for them.[39] The following are some recommended strategies faculty can practice and use.

Create space for difficult exchanges, such as expressing feelings about the exchanges, rather than trying to cover up what happened.[40] Modeling is an important first step, and the instructor could say, for example, "Although I am the professor, I don't have all the answers on this topic, and that is difficult for me" or "I think there is an important point being made, and I don't want to ignore it just because it is uncomfortable. I need time to consider how to respond to this. Thank you for sharing this with me." An acknowledgment that something has happened need not derail a class or lab meeting. If you have to come back to a challenging situation at the start of the next class, consult a colleague with strong cultural competence to serve as a sounding board for ideas on what you can do to return to class prepared. If you have trouble finding a colleague to turn to, this might be a place for a department-level workshop (see Chapter 7).

Realize that defensiveness is a natural reaction to difficult dialogues. When someone does notice that something inappropriate has been said or done and chooses to address it, doing so publicly places the focus on the initiator. Under scrutiny, initiators may feel misunderstood, judged, or shamed.[41] Faculty can set the tone by steering students away from zeroing in on the initiator of a troubling comment and instead use the opportunity to invite discussion (e.g., "I can see everyone is interested in the position that Jason has taken. Let's consider the merits of that position and hear additional input from others.") Depending on the nature of the classroom dynamics, a faculty member may have to de-escalate the situation and employ techniques that combine support with confrontation by taking time out from the group discussion and meeting privately with an initiator instead of pursuing further discussion in front of the class.[42]

Improve communication from the outset by setting norms for classes and lab meetings that include a wide range of techniques such as taking turns to speak. To keep communication open among diverse team members, start a conversation about the group's norms and make sure that members are satisfied with the group interactions and that they are working well for them.[43] For example, you can create a schedule for checking in each week or every two weeks by having students submit a short update on group members' participation that could include reports on whether they are contributing to decisions and if they are following through on tasks. By following such a process, group members can determine concrete actions they can take to promote inclusion. Setting such guidelines beforehand rather than after the fact when there is trouble can prevent problems. Instructors should include directions so students know how to interrupt a process that is not working. For example, some instructors suggest students use a key word such as "Ouch" to signal when something has hit them in a particularly negative way.

Throughout the United States, people are advocating for safe spaces for student learning, but the concept of safety may be confused with a lack of rigor and exceedingly high levels of comfort where everyone feels good about what happens in class. Indeed, the concept of safe spaces was not originally intended to suggest that classrooms strive to be comfortable for everyone or to avoid all conflict.[44] Being safe means students feel respected and recognized, and that they belong and are able to broach difficult topics without fear of being put down or ridiculed. Faculty can promote safe spaces when they develop ground rules for their classes, model how to participate, and provide ways to support ideas or engage in conflict.[45] It is important to take steps to ensure students from all backgrounds feel included and supported in your classroom or lab.

Recovering From a Difficult Exchange or Microaggression in the Classroom

- In this class (or lab), I think it is important to set some ground rules for discussions.
- Although I am the professor, I do not have all the answers. I'll get back to you about this issue during our next class.
- Could we hit the pause button? I would like a chance to rephrase that.
- Let's take a five-minute break and regroup.
- Could you tell me more about how you reached that conclusion?
- Did you mean to use that phrase? Would you please rephrase that? I might not understand your intent.
- Don't forget this week you will be submitting your process checks. I'd love to hear what is or is not working.[46]

The Benefits of Mentor Orientation Sessions and Practice

Throughout this book, we have seen that mentoring comes in many different forms. An orientation helps clarify mentors' roles and specify what they are expected to focus on. All too often, mentors are recruited to serve in a formal program, on a career panel, or as a guest speaker in the class but are not provided with any direction. No one wants to appear disrespectful by subjecting colleagues or guests to some kind of training when they are experts in their field, but many will have no prior formal experience with mentoring. At the same time, your mentors are busy people, so why not respect their time and effort by providing some helpful context? Mentors especially appreciate learning how their messages can be framed for maximum impact for a particular audience. For this reason, I recommend selecting mentors who are open to professional development or coaching to make their participation worthwhile and effective.

The results of your pilot data will be instructive in deciding what to include in an orientation session. Be sure to ask mentors and students to point out where the program did not go as smoothly as they had hoped, what guidance they wish they had received from the orientation session, or at which point they wished they had had additional support. You can ask these questions a month into an initiative or halfway through rather than waiting until the end of a program or a semester. You will be able to fine-tune your program in the future, but you will also collect relevant scenarios to use in future training sessions. MentorNet.org provides effective online training modules for its mentors based on pilot testing.[47]

A segment on implicit bias should be included in your training. The most common tool to raise awareness about implicit bias is Harvard University's Project Implicit (implicit.harvard.edu/implicit) in which individuals can test their unconscious bias, including their preferences based on race or gender. Many people appreciate video simulations or case scenario discussions to provide them with practice when they encounter a situation where a personal bias might surface. To explain implicit bias, the National Aeronautics and Space Administration (NASA) created a resource that provides scenarios that illustrate how job applicants from different races can be perceived or how faculty and staff of different genders may be treated (missionstem.nasa.gov/eLearn.html). Although learning individually is important, it can be helpful to conduct this session in a group so participants have a chance to talk to each other about what they learn. I recommend, for example, including a discussion of implicit bias following a group orientation session in which everyone has viewed the NASA presentation or another similar tool.

Finally, you might draw from additional texts that allow you to practice a range of challenging conversations; for example, *Crucial Conversations*[48] and *Fierce Conversations*[49] are good places to start. You might also choose a book about how people learn, such as Carol Dweck's *Mindset*,[50] or about the role of stereotypes in our lived experiences, such as Claude Steele's *Whistling Vivaldi*.[51]

Reader Next Steps: Invest in Conversations About Difficult Mentoring Moments

The power of mentoring interactions is threatened when we fail to consider the impact of how we frame our messages. While there is no magic formula, the techniques described in this chapter should help you find ways to improve your communication in mentoring. The most important recommendation is to invest in conversations about mentoring messages. And don't skip that orientation session—provide it or attend it, as the case may be.

- Stress your high standards and your belief in students when discussing their performance with them and offer strategies. The next time a student asks you about something out of your area, refer her or him to the appropriate individual or resource.
- Ask guest speakers to include a challenge they overcame as students.

- Consider the role of group norms, particularly in your lab teams or classroom. Is the climate appropriate? Model the ability to pause, ask a question, or rewind a conversation to revise a statement.
- Review pilot data to inform the development of orientation sessions for mentors. Ask about the most challenging situations, and use these to spark discussion and share strategies in future initiatives. Learn more about implicit bias. Watch the NASA implicit bias (missionstem.nasa.gov/eLearn.html) presentation with colleagues and have a discussion about your own lab teams.
- Draw a colleague into one of the conversations you regularly encounter in your work as teachers, advisers, and researchers. Collectively read a relevant book, such as *Crucial Conversations*, *Mindset*, or *Whistling Vivaldi*, as a starting point.
- Don't underestimate the power of reframing a message to a student or during conversations with a colleague about ways to frame feedback you give to students. Gains can be made one student, one colleague, and one interaction at a time.

Notes

1. Tannen, D. (1990). *You just don't understand! Women and men in conversation.* New York, NY: Ballantine.
2. Steele, C. M. (1997). A threat in the air: How stereotypes shape intellectual identity and performance. *American Psychologist, 52*(6), 613–629.
3. Ream, R. K., Lewis, J. L., Echeverria, B., & Page, R. N. (2014). Trust matters: Distinction and diversity in undergraduate science education. *Teachers College Record, 116*(5), 1–50.
4. Constantine M. G., & Sue, D. W. (2007). Perceptions of racial microaggressions among Black supervisees in cross-racial dyads. *Journal of Counseling Psychology, 54*(2), 142–153.
5. Crosby, J. R., & Monin, B. (2007). Failure to warn: The effect of race on warnings of potential academic difficulty. *Journal of Experimental Social Psychology, 43*(4), 663–670.
6. Rattan, A., Good, C., & Dweck, C. S. (2012). "It's ok—not everyone can be good at math": Instructors with an entity theory comfort (and demotivate) students. *Journal of Experimental Social Psychology, 48*(3), 731–737.
7. Cohen, G. L., Steele, C. M., & Ross, L. D. (1999). The mentor's dilemma: Providing critical feedback across the racial divide. *Personality and Social Psychology Bulletin, 25*, 1302–1318.
8. Rattan, A., Good, C., & Dweck, C. S. (2012). "It's ok—not everyone can be good at math": Instructors with an entity theory comfort (and demotivate) students. *Journal of Experimental Social Psychology, 48*(3), 731–737.

9. Cialdini, R. B. (2001). *Influence: Science and practice.* Boston, MA: Allyn & Bacon.

10. Cohen, G. L., Steele, C. M., & Ross, L. D. (1999). The mentor's dilemma: Providing critical feedback across the racial divide. *Personality and Social Psychology Bulletin, 25*(10), 1302–1318; Rattan, A., Good, C., & Dweck, C. S. (2012). "It's ok—not everyone can be good at math": Instructors with an entity theory comfort (and demotivate) students. *Journal of Experimental Social Psychology, 48,* 731–737.

11. Hoyt, C. L. (2013). Inspirational or self-deflating: The role of self-efficacy in elite role model effectiveness. *Social Psychological and Personality Science,* 4(3), 290–298.

12. Lockwood, P., & Kunda, Z. (1997). Superstars and me: Predicting the impact of role models on the self. *Journal of Personality and Social Psychology, 73*(1), 91–103.

13. Bandura, A., & Schunk, D. H. (1981). Cultivating competence, self-efficacy, and intrinsic interest through proximal self-motivation. *Journal of Personality and Social Psychology, 41,* 586–598.

14. Schunk, D. H. (1991). Self-efficacy and academic motivation. *Educational Psychologist, 26*(3/4), 207–231.

15. Stephens, N. M., Hamedani, M. G., & Destin, M. (2014). Closing the social-class achievement gap: A difference-education intervention improves first-generation students' academic performance and all students' college transition. *Psychological Science, 25*(4), 943–953.

16. Packard, B. W., & Hudgings, J. H. (2002). Expanding college women's perceptions of physicists' lives and work through interactions with a physics careers web site. *Journal of College Science Teaching, 32*(3), 164–170.

17. Packard, B. W. (2003). Web-based mentoring: Challenging traditional models to increase women's access. *Mentoring & Tutoring: Partnerships in Learning, 11*(1), 53–65.

18. Asgari, S., Dasgupta, N., & Stout, J. G. (2012). When do counterstereotypic ingroup members inspire vs. deflate? The effect of successful professional women on women's leadership self-concept. *Personality and Social Psychology Bulletin, 38(3),* 370–383.

19. Packard, B. W. (2003). Student training promotes mentoring awareness and action. *Career Development Quarterly, 51*(4), 335–345.

20. Hoyt, C. L. (2013). Inspirational or self-deflating: The role of self-efficacy in elite role model effectiveness. *Social Psychological and Personality Science,* 4(3), 290–298.

21. Mann, S. J. (2001). Alternative perspectives on the student experience: Alienation and engagement. *Studies in Higher Education, 26*(1), 7–19.

22. Packard, B. W., & Jeffers, K. (2013). Advising and progress in the community college STEM transfer pathway. *NACADA Journal, 33*(2), 65–75.

23. Packard, B. W., & Jeffers, K. (2013). Advising and progress in the community college STEM transfer pathway. *NACADA Journal, 33*(2), 65–75.

24. Pierce, C. M. (1995). Stress analogs of racism and sexism: Terrorism, torture, and disaster. In C. V. Willie, P. P. Ricker, B. M. Kramer, & B. S. Brown (Eds.),

Mental health, racism, and sexism (pp. 277–293). Pittsburgh, PA: University of Pittsburgh Press, p. 281.

25. Sue, D. W., Bucceri, J., Lin, A. I., Nadal, K. L., & Torino, G. C. (2007). Racial microaggressions and the Asian American experience. *Cultural Diversity and Ethnic Minority Psychology, 13*(1), 72–81.

26. Yosso, T. Y., Smith, W. A., Ceja, M., & Solorzano, D. G. (2009). Critical race theory, racial microaggressions, and campus racial climate for Latino/a undergraduates. *Harvard Educational Review, 79*(4), 659–690.

27. Schoulte, J. C., Schultz, J. M., & Altmaier, E. M. (2011). Forgiveness in response to cultural microaggressions. *Counselling Psychology Quarterly, 24*(4), 291–300.

28. Sue, D. W. (2010). *Microaggressions in everyday life: Race, gender, and sexual orientation.* Hoboken, NJ: Wiley.

29. Smith, W. A., Hung, M., & Franklin, J. D. (2011). Racial battle fatigue and the miseducation of Black men: Racial microaggressions, societal programs, and environmental stress. *Journal of Negro Education, 80*(1), 63–82.

30. Turner, C. S. V., Gonzales, J. C., & Wood, J. L. (2008). Faculty of color in academe: What 20 years of literature tells us. *Journal of Diversity in Higher Education, 1*(3), 139–168.

31. Gomez, M. L., Khurshid, A., Freitag, M. B., & Lachuk, A. J. (2011). Microaggressions in graduate students' lives: How they are encountered and their consequences. *Teaching and Teacher Education, 27*(8), 1189–1199.

32. Sue, D. W., Capodilupo, C. M., Nadal, K. L., & Torino, G. C. (2008). Racial microaggressions and the power to define reality. *American Psychologist, 63*(4), 277–279.

33. Quaye, S. J. (2014). Facilitating dialogues about racial realities. *Teachers College Record, 116*(8), 1–42.

34. Solorzano, D., Ceja, M., & Yosso, T. (2000). Critical race theory, racial microaggressions, and campus racial climate: The experiences of African American college students. *Journal of Negro Education, 69*(1/2), 60–73.

35. Watt, S. K., (2007). Difficult dialogues and social justice: Use of the privileged identity exploration (PIE) model in student affairs practice. *College Student Affairs Journal, 26*(2), 114–126.

36. Pasque, P. A, Chesler, M. A, Charbeneau, J., & Carlson, C. (2013). Pedagogical approaches to student racial conflict in the classroom. *Journal of Diversity in Higher Education, 6*(1), 1–16.

37. Boysen, G. A., & Vogel, D. L. (2009). Bias in the classroom: Types, frequencies, and responses. *Teaching of Psychology, 36*(1), 12–17; Jackson, S. M., Hillard, A. L., & Schneider, T. R. (2014). Using implicit bias training to improve attitudes toward women in STEM. *Social Psychology of Education, 17*(3), 419–438.

38. Sue, D. W. (2013). Race talk: The psychology of racial dialogues. *American Psychologist, 68*(8), 663–672.

39. Miner-Rubino, K., & Cortina, L. M. (2007). Beyond targets: Consequences of vicarious exposure to misogyny at work. *Journal of Applied Psychology, 92*(5), 1254–1269.

40. Sue, D. W., Rivera, D. P., Watkins, N. L., Kim, R. H., Kim, S., & Williams, C. D. (2011). Racial dialogues: Challenges faculty of color face in the classroom. *Cultural Diversity and Ethnic Minority Psychology*, *17*(3), 331–340.

41. Loschiavo, C., Miller, D. S., & Davies, J. (2007). Engaging men in difficult dialogues about privilege. *College Student Affairs Journal*, *26*(2), 193–200.

42. Burton, S., & Furr, S. (2014). Conflict in multicultural classes: Approaches to resolving difficult dialogues. *Counselor Education & Supervision*, *53*(2), 97–110.

43. Zúñiga, X., Nagda, B. A., Chesler, M., & Cytron-Walker, A. (2007). Intergroup dialogue in higher education: Meaningful learning about social justice. *ASHE Higher Education Report*, *32*(4), 1–128.

44. Boostrom, R. (1998). "Safe spaces": Reflections on an educational metaphor. *Journal of Curriculum Studies*, *30*(4), 397–408.

45. Holley, L. C., & Steiner, S. (2005). Safe space: Student perspectives on classroom environment. *Journal of Social Work Education*, *41*(1), 49–64.

46. Burton, S., & Furr, S. (2014). Conflict in multicultural classes: Approaches to resolving difficult dialogues. *Counselor Education & Supervision*, *53*(2), 97–110; Sue, D. W. (2013). Race talk: The psychology of racial dialogues. *American Psychologist*, *68*(8), 663–672; Zúñiga, X., Nagda, B. A., Chesler, M., & Cytron-Walker, A. (2007). Intergroup dialogue in higher education: Meaningful learning about social justice. *ASHE Higher Education Report*, *32*(4), 1–128.

47. Kasprisin, C. A., Boyle Single, P., Single, R. M., & Muller, C. B. (2003). Building a better bridge: Testing e-training to improve e-mentoring programs for diversity in higher education. *Mentoring & Tutoring*, *11*(1), 67–78.

48. Patterson, K., Grenny, J., McMillan, R., & Switzler, A. (2002). *Crucial conversations*. New York, NY: McGraw-Hill.

49. Scott, S. (2002). *Fierce conversations*. New York, NY: Viking.

50. Dweck, C. S. (2006). *Mindset: The new psychology of success*. New York, NY: Random House.

51. Steele, C. (2011). *Whistling Vivaldi: How stereotypes affect us and what we can do*. New York, NY: Norton.

7

CONVERSATIONS AMONG COLLEAGUES

Departmental Climate as a Collective Project

This book focuses on ways to improve the mentoring and persistence of underrepresented students in STEM fields. I have discussed many mentoring approaches as well as ways to frame messages effectively to maximize impact. In this chapter, I take a closer look at the departmental climate. The title of Freeman Hrabowski's book says it all: *Change Institutional Culture, and You Change Who Goes Into Science.*[1] Indeed, the climate, or departmental culture, influences the capacity, interest, and belongingness of students because the climate reflects the energy and temperature of the department. We can sense climates that are encouraging, warm, and energetic and that tell us we are capable and will be supported, invite us to participate, or value us as members of the community. We can also sense toxic, chilly, or stagnant climates that suggest conditions not ripe for growth.

Because we are all different—some of us wear T-shirts or long-sleeve shirts when others need overcoats—addressing departmental climate can be challenging. Some people find the climate to be just right, whereas others see issues that need to be resolved. The biggest challenge, then, is how to raise awareness about climate issues and understand that our own sense of contentment may not reflect how others feel. Thus, climate is not just about the students. Climate permeates the department in very tangible ways that influence everyone working there.

Climate is also important because even the best-designed initiatives can be counteracted by negative messages embedded in the department. At the same time, well-designed mentoring initiatives can be bolstered by a department climate that provides inclusive cues and messages. We can understand and change the climate by focusing on particular indicators, asking ourselves if these indicators reflect the messages we want, and if not, will we commit to changing them to achieve a different outcome?

Changing Climate, One Conversation at a Time

In this chapter, my goal is to help you find a way to start worthwhile conversations about departmental climate as a collective project. Conversations can help us identify discrepancies between the actual reputation of our department and our idealized versions. We can commit to looking candidly at the climates in our departments for opportunities to improve.

Throughout this book, I focus on three interconnected indicators of departmental climate: representation, reputation, and resources (e.g., see Chapter 1, pp. 19–20), and in this chapter I suggest ways to initiate conversations focused on each of these indicators.

- *Representation* refers to diversity in the department, including the people in the department, how they got there, and whether they decide to stay. The hiring process affects representation.
- *Reputation* refers to whether students see your department as an inclusive, energetic place to learn and thrive. Does your department convey the ethos or temperature you would like to see? Teaching and advising, including professional development, influence departmental reputation.
- *Resource allocation and policies* influence whether and how your resources align with your commitments.

I close the chapter by helping you plan a departmental conversation, whether with one colleague or the whole department.

Representation and Departmental Hiring Processes

The composition of the department matters; thus, so do the hiring processes for STEM faculty and staff. The low numbers of women and people of color working in STEM departments are stark, especially for faculty. Representation of people from diverse backgrounds is one indicator of inclusivity in a department. However, this can be a catch-22 when a department is not diverse to begin with and faces the challenge to recruit people with diverse backgrounds. Not all diversity is visible (e.g., class background or even race), which limits the ways of knowing a department's true composition and how commitments toward diversity are interpreted.

How do you improve the recruitment and retention of people from diverse backgrounds to work in your departments? Fortunately, many excellent resources exist that walk you through diversifying hiring pools and reducing the impact of implicit bias.[2] While a department works on diversifying its faculty and staff, conversations are essential but sometimes painful. For example, a department administrator may need to address the reasons underrepresentation of diverse faculty exists. Not everyone wants to undertake a deep examination of implicit bias or discuss a climate study examining whether and how a department is or is not inclusive. In some cases, a department will hire one woman or person of color and then revert to its old practices of recruitment and hiring. In other cases, department administrators put all their energy into hiring without recognizing the need for resources in continued professional development for all department members. The students aren't the only ones who struggle when a senior faculty member or department chair lacks the knowledge or the skill to disrupt bias or create supportive environments for diverse learners. Indeed, the lone underrepresented faculty or staff member can be overburdened with requests for mentoring from students and with insensitive comments from colleagues.[3]

Pick any avenue to start a conversation about hiring processes, from the recruitment of new faculty to supporting ongoing professional development. The department's or institution's offerings in terms of professional development can communicate different messages to new hires about the departmental climate. The more professional development programs include bias literacy and leadership development, the more visible a department's commitments to creating a positive climate are. National professional organizations committed to diversity in STEM are great places to start looking for resources. A department's commitment to diversity will appear more authentic if current faculty discuss their participation in development opportunities and associated resources of these organizations with potential hires.

A diversity and inclusion statement issued by the department can prevent job candidates from assuming that the department has a color-blind philosophy. Application materials can include a request for all candidates to describe their commitment to teaching and mentoring a diverse student body and to engage in this conversation during the application process, which brings all candidates into the conversation.[4]

Conversation Starters: Hiring Process

Discuss with colleagues implicit bias and the steps the department will take to limit its effects before composing the job advertisement.[5] Commit to discussing the attributes of ideal candidates before reviewing job applications by using the following or a similar conversation starter:[6]

> I know we have time pressures, but let's talk first about the characteristics of the ideal candidates. I know we all have good intentions, and, because of that, I am sure that reading this article about how we can limit implicit bias will help us in our process.

Broaden your search pool using a multipronged approach, and evaluate the efficacy of your strategy after each search:[7]

> How have our efforts to diversify our search pools been working? Our peers attend a national meeting to recruit, even when they do not have an open position. Should we?

> Let's read Christopher Lee's book or Daryl Smith's book to see if there is a strategy we want to try.[8]

Talk openly and candidly about the position requirements, including written and unwritten parts of the job, and what kinds of responsibilities you all share.

> What will it mean for this new hire to teach the same course as our most senior faculty member? Also, this hire will have the largest number of students in the department. Let's discuss equity.

Departmental Reputation for Teaching and Advising

To change its reputation, department members might need to reboot their central assumptions to reflect an ethos of inclusivity. As Carl Wieman observed, institutions should shift from talent identification to talent development, which means that STEM departments typically sift through students looking for talent rather than regarding students as talent ready to be cultivated through teaching and advising.[9] We know that the approachability of faculty and staff also influences climate; when students know they can ask questions and that faculty believe in them, the overall departmental reputation is enhanced.[10]

Furthermore, departmental practices need to better align with what we know about how students learn. For decades, researchers have demonstrated that active learning promotes deeper learning and engagement.[11] Yet lectures still dominate in classrooms.[12] Even though many faculty say they want to see critical thinking and robust application of knowledge, many assessments are limited to surface-level recall.[13] Many departments face barriers to change; for example, they may lack resources to invest in more systematic changes. And yet some departments have managed to shift energy and resources so they are more effective, reaping positive benefits for not only students but also the department as a whole. Seeking to improve the department's reputation as a collective project helps illustrate the shared benefits of engaging in pedagogical innovations.

Although individual faculty members can have an impact by changing teaching practices, we know that transformative change is more likely when many members of a department do this together.[14] When faculty have a chance to participate in a learning community rather than a one-time workshop, they are more likely to commit to goals, engage in systematic study and inquiry, and make changes that last in the long run.[15] Faculty benefit from peer-to-peer feedback.[16] They also appreciate talking to each other about their inquiry into teaching and learning.[17]

Some faculty start with a reading group focusing on the latest research in active learning or scientific teaching. The group can start by reading books or articles from leaders in this area such as Jo Handelsman or Sylvia Hurtado. For example, I recommend *Scientific Teaching* by Handelsman as a catalyst for action.[18] Others might benefit from the information on the ENGAGE Engineering website (engageengineering.org) and committing to implement a real-world example into each week's class that semester. Department members might also benefit from participating in a curricular mapping exercise to see how all the department's courses fit together.[19]

You may find it useful to invite an outside expert to campus to spark a conversation. Or you might send a colleague to a national institute or focused meeting. Project Kaleidoscope's summer institutes for faculty leadership (www.aacu.org/pkal) is an excellent choice, and the American Association of Colleges & Universities sponsors additional conferences focused on STEM and diversity (see also www.aacu.org/pkal/events). Attending a conference to kick off or maintain ongoing learning for you and your colleagues can help increase the chances of making progress as a department.

Does *everyone* need to be on board? Starting with one or a few colleagues, see if you can garner enough interest to develop a department-level plan. By starting the conversation, you can find out whether a new initiative you designed is representative of the department or contrasts with the prevailing norms. If innovation is rare and in contrast to the norms, then the effectiveness of an innovative initiative will likely be diminished in the long run.

Conversation Starters: Reputation

Talk about your department's reputation and whether it reflects what you would like to see, for example:

- I have heard people say we have enough students in our major. Why do we say that? I'm concerned that we are not looking at why some students leave.
- I know we are proud of our scholar program. How do students who are not in the scholar program feel about our department? How do we bridge this gap in experience?
- Let's read *Scientific Teaching* together.[20] I think it will help us with our struggles regarding our introductory sequence.
- How can we improve the approachability of the faculty and staff in our department?
- What messages are we sending during advising sessions?

Alignment of Resources With Commitments

How a department spends its money and staff time is an important decision. Department heads make decisions at the beginning of each budget cycle and each day on how to allocate scarce resources. Questions during the decision-making process may include the following:

- Why spend money on a department lecture series but not on faculty mentoring? Is there a way to combine these initiatives?
- If academic support resources such as supplemental instruction make a difference in one course, should we consider ways to allocate resources to another course?
- If the time spent in office hours or in departmental meetings is not effective, how can this time be used more effectively?
- If current resource allocations are not effective, could allocations be changed to improve their impact?

Consider some additional ways to think more about how you are allocating resources. Look at institutions and their departments that have undergone transformation for new ideas for your department. The ADVANCE program sponsored by the NSF (www.nsf.gov/funding/pgm_summ.jsp?pims_id=5383) provides many excellent examples of ways institutions have transformed to make their climates more supportive for women faculty. Many of these strategies can be adapted for other groups, such as people of color. For example, proactive and targeted mentoring efforts can increase competencies and raise awareness of department chairs so they can take action and reduce the isolation or exclusion of women.[21] A booklet on the ADVANCE program at North Dakota State University, which is called the FORWARD program (www.ndsu.edu/forward), contains the photos, names, and departments of male allies who completed specialized ally and advocate training in regard to implicit bias, departmental climate, and support for women colleagues; this provides a visual recognition of commitment at the department and individual level. The ADVANCE program at Northeastern University offered colleagues the chance to learn about how to be an effective diversity ally on a search committee (www.northeastern.edu/advance). Even if you don't have an active grant, you can still find out more by talking to someone who is familiar with the program.

Other organizations offering resources include the Women in Engineering ProActive Network (wepan.org), which sponsors an annual conference with excellent professional development opportunities for people who want to learn more about the issues facing women in engineering and to build relevant skills. For example, participants can learn how to speak up or intervene when they observe bias in the workplace by using active bystander techniques (e.g., see www.simmons.edu/about-simmons/centers-organizations-and-institutes/cgo/services/bystander-awareness-training). The National Center for Women & Information Technology (www.ncwit.org) has many resources, including affinity memberships to help with networking. The Society for the Advancement of Chicanos & Native Americans in Science (sacnas.org) also offers valuable resources and hosts an annual conference.

For the liberal arts environment, the Liberal Arts College Association for Faculty Inclusion (web.grinnell.edu/science/lacafi) offers a network to share ideas, and the Consortium for Faculty Diversity in Liberal Arts Colleges (www.gettysburg.edu/about/offices/provost/cfd) sponsors an annual conference for aspiring academics and senior faculty mentors alike. In addition, the Higher Education Recruitment Consortium (www.hercjobs.org) offers regional meetings focused on diversity. As previously mentioned, Project Kaleidoscope holds the Summer Leadership Institute for STEM Faculty, and the American Association of Colleges & Universities sponsors additional conferences. In summary, although many resources are available, not all departments have allocated funds to take advantage of them. Develop an action plan for your department, or check with the institution's entity that receives regular updates on available resources to avoid missing out on regular opportunities to learn.

Conversation Starters: Resource Allocations

Start by examining the allocation of department resources for things that do work:

- We currently allocate academic support for Biology 1. Is it possible to expand this to Biology 2 or 3? Where would we need to make cuts in our budget in order to start doing that?

Draw attention to any discrepancies as a way to start the conversation:

- I notice we always pride ourselves on being an inclusive department. Is there a reason we do not have a Women in Science chapter or that we do not cohost an event for Black history month?
- A peer institution with fewer resources just completed an ADVANCE grant. Let's invite people from that campus to talk about what they are doing.

Track Your Progress

You can gain a sense of the departmental climate by evaluating any adjustments you have made. Consider whether or how those changes affected students, staff, and faculty in your department. For example, if students repeatedly cite the lack of diversity in the department, you might consider creating a plan that strategically improves your hiring processes and commit to a time line for assessing the impact of your efforts. Let's say you developed an initiative that allows students to attend the annual meeting of a national organization and found that the students valued that experience and think differently about the department as a result. You might choose to develop similar initiatives in the same spirit.

Reader Next Steps: Plan Your Department Conversation

In this chapter I suggest a number of conversations. Consider introducing a conversation that might help the department as a whole take a step forward.

- Think about a colleague who might share your interest in an area as a place to start for a conversation. If you both have an array of interests, focusing on one or two overlapping areas of shared interest can help.

- Discuss how you allocate resources to invest in mentoring or a more inclusive department during your next departmental meeting.
- Consider whether your department has interdivisional or collegewide retreats that might present an opportunity for a broader conversation among colleagues.
- Consider inviting guests from other campuses who are highly regarded and knowledgeable about transforming the departmental climate.
- Don't underestimate the power of starting the conversation, one colleague at a time.

Notes

1. Hrabowski, F. A., & Maton, K. I. (2009). *Change institutional culture, and you change who goes into science.* Washington, DC: American Association of University Professors.

2. Lee, C. D. (2014). *A comprehensive guide to successful faculty, staff, and administrative searches* (2nd ed.). Sterling, VA: Stylus; Smith, D. G. (2009). *Diversity's promise for higher education: Making it work.* Baltimore, MD: Johns Hopkins University Press.

3. Rockquemore, K., & Laszloffy, T. (2008). *The Black academic's guide to winning tenure—without losing your soul.* Boulder, CO: Lynne Rienner.

4. Purdie-Vaughns, V., Steele, C. M., Davies, P. G., Ditlmann, R., & Crosby, J. R. (2008). Social identity contingencies: How diversity cues signal threat or safety for African Americans in mainstream institutions. *Journal of Personality and Social Psychology, 94*(4), 615–630.

5. Carnes, M., Devine, P. G., Isaac, C., Manwell, L. B., Ford, C. E., Byars-Winston, A., . . . Sheridan, J. (2012). Promoting institutional change through bias literacy. *Journal of Diversity in Higher Education, 5*(2), 63–77.

6. Uhlmann, E., & Cohen, G. L. (2005). Constructed criteria: Redefining merit to justify discrimination. *Psychological Science, 16*(6), 474–480.

7. Smith, D. G. (2009). *Diversity's promise for higher education: Making it work.* Baltimore, MD: Johns Hopkins University Press.

8. Lee, C. D. (2014). *Search committees: A comprehensive guide to successful faculty, staff, and administrative searches.* Sterling, VA: Stylus; Smith, D. G. (2009). *Diversity's promise for higher education: Making it work.* Baltimore, MD: Johns Hopkins University Press.

9. Mervis, J. (2013). Transformation is possible if a university really cares. *Science, 340*(6130), 292–296.

10. Hurtado, S., Eagan, M. K., Tran, M. C., Newman, C. B., Chang, M. J., & Velasco, P. (2013). "We do science here": Underrepresented students' interactions with faculty in different college contexts. *Journal of Social Issues, 67*(3), 553–579.

11. Walker, J. D., Cotner, S. H., Baepler, P. M., & Decker, M. D. (2008). A delicate balance: Integrating active learning into a large lecture course. *CBE–Life Sciences Education, 7*(4), 361–367.

12. Mervis, J. (2010). Undergraduate science: Better intro courses seen as key to reducing attrition of STEM majors. *Science, 330*(6002), 306.

13. Crowe, A., Dirks, C., & Wenderoth, M. P. (2008). Biology in bloom: Implementing Bloom's taxonomy to enhance student learning in biology. *CBE–Life Sciences Education, 7*(4), 368–381.

14. Breslow, L. (2010). Wrestling with pedagogical change: The TEAL initiative at MIT. *Change, 42*(5), 23–29.

15. Addis, E. A., Quardokus, K. M., Bassham, D. C., Becraft, P. W., Boury, N., Coffman, C. R., . . . Powell-Coffman, J. (2013). Implementing pedagogical change in introductory biology courses through the use of faculty learning communities. *Journal of College Science Teaching, 43*(2), 22–29.

16. Gormally, C., Evans, M., & Brickman, P. (2014). Feedback about teaching in higher ed: Neglected opportunities to promote change. *CBE–Life Sciences Education, 13*(2), 187–199.

17. Moore, J. A., & Carter-Hicks, J. (2014). Let's talk! Facilitating a faculty learning community using a critical friends group approach. *International Journal for the Scholarship of Teaching & Learning, 8*(2), 1–17.

18. Handelsman, J., Miller, S., & Pfund, C. (2006). *Scientific teaching.* New York, NY: W. H. Freeman.

19. Breslow, L. (2010). Wrestling with pedagogical change: The TEAL initiative at MIT. *Change, 42*(5), 23–29.

20. Handelsman, J., Miller, S., & Pfund, C. (2006). *Scientific teaching.* New York, NY: W. H. Freeman.

21. Handelsman, J., Cantor, N., Carnes, M., Denton, D., Fine, E., Grosz, B., & Sheridan, J. (2005). More women in science. *Science, 309*(5738), 1190–1191.

CONCLUSION

In this book, I focus on the power of mentoring to support the persistence of students from underrepresented backgrounds including women, first-generation college students, students of color, and community-college transfer students, among others. You are more likely to produce results when you organize mentoring intentionally by implementing many different types of approaches that include programs, events, policies, and core practices of advising and teaching. We need to think about not only individual students but also our learning environments and departmental climates. We can fine-tune how messages are framed to maximize impact, and we need to work together as faculty, staff, and department chairs to take on the challenge of student persistence.

Start Small

We mapped out the big picture, which revealed an enormous number of obstacles that can be daunting to face, let alone overcome. I hope I have convinced you that you can start small, wherever you are, with whatever resources you have. This can mean trying a new way to organize or improve your peer mentoring or provide critical feedback. Or you might try to invite colleagues to join you in a conversation about hiring or resource allocations. Whatever you do, be sure to track your progress, and see if your efforts are contributing to the outcomes you seek.

The Tipping Point

Small changes can have a big impact; they can add up and tip the balance for your department. As Malcolm Gladwell observed, the tipping point is dependent on a range of factors and varies with context.[1] Your tipping point might be the third colleague you tap for a conversation about the energy in the department. It might be the eighth classroom in which you implement active learning with quality feedback, or it could be when your department starts a local chapter of a national organization. I don't wish to underestimate what it takes to create real change, and yet I want to encourage you to take steps that move you forward.

Who Do You Want to Be?

Although we are constrained by departmental budgets and institutional policies, we are also constrained by our own ways of doing things. If we do not allocate time to talk about the curriculum collectively or talk candidly about our current mentoring programs and how they are working, then we are not going to move forward.

Investing in mentoring benefits us all. Effectively mentoring a new colleague or a student often contributes to empowerment, new skills, or a stronger sense of belonging. In turn, mentors also feel more effective. And when our departments are diverse and inclusive and have a strong reputation for mentoring the next generation, we are also proud of that achievement.

We live and work in the culture we create. What we do for our students, we do for ourselves. By focusing on our mentoring initiatives and investing in them to make them more powerful, we invest in our potential to create change and create a generation of STEM graduates who are proud of their departments, institutions, and disciplines. I am excited to hear about your next steps. I hope you will find the resources presented in this book helpful as you continue moving forward in this important work of supporting mentoring, diversity, and persistence.

Remember: one student, one colleague, one interaction at a time.

Reader Next Steps: Summarize What You Have Learned

Consider sharing the following steps with a colleague:

- Map your departmental or institutional landscape to see the big picture of STEM persistence.
- Choose a focus, and learn more from the data you have.
- Review a range of mentoring approaches, and try something.
- Pilot your efforts, track your progress, and refine your plans.
- Include orientation and practice for mentors, and improve efforts by reviewing pilot data.
- Practice framing messages to students with your colleagues.

- Talk to your colleagues about the departmental climate for under-represented students.
- Invite colleagues to read an important book together, and plan collective action.
- Track your resources and your overall progress; refine your plans.
- Remember: one student, one colleague, one interaction at a time.

Note

1. Gladwell, M. (2006). *The tipping point: How little things can make a big difference*. Boston, MA: Little, Brown.

RESOURCES

Professional Organizations and Consortia

American Association for University Women, aauw.org
American Society for Engineering Education, www.asee.org
Association for Women in Science, www.awis.org
Consortium for Faculty Diversity in Liberal Arts Colleges, www.gettysburg.edu/
    about/offices/provost/cfd
Higher Education Recruitment Consortium, www.hercjobs.org
Liberal Arts College Association for Faculty Inclusion, web.grinnell.edu/science/lacafi
National Association of Diversity Officers in Higher Education, www.nadohe.org
National Organization for the Professional Advancement of Black Chemists and
    Chemical Engineers, www.nobcche.org
National Research Mentoring Network, www.nrmnet.net
Society of Black Engineers, www.nsbe.org
Society for Chicanos and Native Americans in Science, sacnas.org
Society of Women Engineers, societyofwomenengineers.swe.org
Southern Regional Education Board, www.sreb.org

Statistics, Strategies, and Tool Kits

ADVANCE, www.portal.advance.vt.edu
Anita Borg Institute, anitaborg.org
Catalyst, www.catalyst.org
ENGAGE Engineering, www.engageengineering.org
Howard Hughes Medical Institute, www.hhmi.org/educational-materials
Institute for Higher Education Policy, www.ihep.org
MentorNet, mentornet.org
Million Women Mentors, www.millionwomenmentors.org
National Academic Advising Association, www.nacada.ksu.edu
National Alliance for Partnerships in Equity, www.napequity.org
National Center for Science and Engineering Statistics, nsf.gov/statistics
National Center for Women and Information Technology, www.ncwit.org
National Institute for Women in Trades, Technology and Science, www.iwitts.org
National Institutes of Health, edi.nih.gov/data/resources
National Research Council, www.nationalacademies.org/nrc
National Science Board, www.nsf.gov/nsb
Project Implicit, implicit.harvard.edu/implicit
Project Kaleidoscope, www.aacu.org/pkal

STEMconnector, www.stemconnector.org
Women in Engineering ProActive Network, www.wepan.org
Yale Center for Scientific Teaching, cst.yale.edu

Recommended Books and Reports

Underrepresented Students

Davis, J. (2010). *The first generation student experience: Implications for campus practice, and strategies for improving persistence and success.* Sterling, VA: Stylus.
Reviews the primary obstacles facing first-generation college students, reviews academic literature, and presents student narratives. Several recommendations for campuses are included.

Hill, C., Corbett, C., & St. Rose, A. (2010). *Why so few women in science, engineering, and mathematics?* Washington, DC: American Association of University Women.
Presents key research findings that pertain to the underrepresentation of women in STEM fields.

Lee, E., & LaDousa, C. (Eds.) (2015). *College students' experiences of power and marginality: Sharing spaces and negotiating differences.* New York, NY: Routledge.
Details the college navigation experiences of students from differing socioeconomic, gender, and racial/ethnic backgrounds and provides strategies for institutions and faculty alike.

Museus, S. D., Palmer, R. T., Davis, R. J., & Maramba, D. (2011). *Racial and ethnic minority student success in STEM education.* San Francisco, CA: Jossey-Bass.
Provides an overview of K–12 and university-level factors influencing the progress of students of color and includes culturally relevant pedagogy, campus culture, and support programs.

National Academies Press. (2011). *Expanding underrepresented minority participation: America's science and technology talent at the crossroads.* Washington, DC: Author.
Documents academic, social, and economic factors contributing to the underrepresentation of racial-ethnic minority students in STEM and makes recommendations for various stakeholders.

Wolverton, A., & Nagaoka, L. (2014). *Breaking in: Women's accounts of how choices shape STEM careers.* Sterling, VA: Stylus.
Provides case studies of successful women in STEM in academia, industry, and government who reflect on the motivators, facilitators, and barriers to their progress.

Teaching, Learning, and Motivation

Ambrose, S. A., Bridges, M. W., DiPietro, M., Lovett, M. C., & Norman, M. K. (2010). *How learning works: Seven research-based principles for smart teaching.* San Francisco: Jossey Bass.
Summarizes what cognitive science has to say about how people learn and effective teaching.

Berardo, K., & Deardorff, D. K. (2012). *Building cultural competence: Innovative activities and models.* Sterling VA: Stylus.

A tool kit to guide trainers in the development of cultural competence in the workplace.

Bowen, J. (2012). *Teaching naked: How moving technology out of your classroom will improve student learning.* San Francisco, CA: Jossey-Bass.

Helps instructors reflect on when to use technology and why to meet particular goals, including ways to promote active learning and comprehension.

Dweck, C. S. (2006). *Mindset: The new psychology of success.* New York, NY: Random House.

Learn more about the growth mind-set and ways to cultivate it in yourself and others.

Handelsman, J., Miller, S., & Pfund, C. (2006). *Scientific teaching.* New York, NY: W. H. Freeman.

Explains ways to study the impact of your teaching with a focus on goals and evidence.

Laursen, S., Hunter, A-B, Seymour, S., Thiry, H., & Melton, G. (2010). *Undergraduate research in the sciences: Engaging students in real science.* San Francisco, CA: Jossey-Bass.

An excellent guide to developing and improving undergraduate research.

Patterson, K., Grenny, J., McMillan, R., & Switzler, A. (2002). *Crucial conversations.* New York, NY: McGraw-Hill.

Insights into why some conversations are difficult and important, and ways to frame messages effectively.

Persellin, D. C., & Daniels, M. B. (2014). *A concise guide to improving student learning: Six evidence-based principles and how to apply them.* Sterling, VA: Stylus.

A guidebook for college instructors that includes insight into metacognition, a useful annotated bibliography, and teaching strategies.

Scott, S. (2002). *Fierce conversations.* New York, NY: Viking.

Offers advice on starting difficult conversations, such as one-on-one performance conversations, constructively and effectively.

Sibley, J., & Ostafichuk, P. (2014). *Getting started with team-based learning.* Sterling, VA: Stylus.

A guidebook that explains how team-based learning works and includes a helpful set of steps to get started.

Stone, D., & Heen, S. (2014). *Thanks for the feedback: The science and art of receiving feedback well.* New York, NY: Viking.

Research and techniques on providing feedback that can be incorporated to minimize defensiveness.

Implicit Bias, Hiring, and Diversity

Banaji, M. R., & Greenwald, A. G. (2013). *Blindspot: Hidden biases of good people.* New York: Random House.

The developers of the implicit association test share what they have learned from millions of people about implicit bias.

Dean, D. J., & Koster, J. B. (2014). *Equitable solutions for retaining a robust STEM workforce: Beyond best practices.* Oxford, UK: Elsevier.

Reviews an array of workplace policies that help retain women in STEM, with a focus on family-friendly policies, mentoring, and implicit bias in the workplace.

Gutierrez y Muhs, G., Niemann, Y. F., Gonzales, C. G., & Harris, A P. (Eds.). (2012). *Presumed incompetent: The intersections of race and class for women in academia.* Boulder, CO: Utah State University Press.

More than 40 contributors share data and lived experiences in the academy, emphasizing the intersections of race, gender, and class, and implications for higher education institutions.

Lee, C. D. (2014). *Search committees: A comprehensive guide to successful faculty, staff, and administrative searches.* Sterling, VA: Stylus.

Includes step-by-step guides, case studies, tools, and templates to help search committees improve their effectiveness.

Page, S. (2008). *The difference: How the power of diversity creates better groups, firms, schools, and societies.* Princeton, NJ: Princeton University Press.

Provides comprehensive research that documents the benefits of diverse teams and practical applications of the research in an array of scenarios.

Ross, H. J. (2014). *Everyday bias: Identifying and navigating unconscious judgments in our daily lives.* Lanham, MD: Rowman & Littlefield.

Explains why everyone is susceptible to bias. Includes exercises for individuals and workplaces to improve awareness and change patterns of interactions.

Smith, D. G. (2009). *Diversity's promise for higher education: Making it work.* Baltimore, MD: Johns Hopkins University Press.

A comprehensive guide to challenges facing higher education institutions working on diversifying their faculty that includes strategies for improvement.

Steele, C. (2011). *Whistling Vivaldi: How stereotypes affect us and what we can do.* New York, NY: Norton.

Synthesizes research concerning the powerful impact of stereotypes, including how stereotypes shape expectations and performance.

INDEX

summer, 13, 36–37, 61–65,
73–74, 94
research-based best practices, 1, 40
Research Experience for
Undergraduates, 84
residential communities, 48
resources, 19, 54. *See also* budgets;
funding
commitment aligning with, 20,
116–17, 120–22
feedback as, 12–14
grants in, 55–56, 73, 75, 93–94
investing of, 35, 39–40, 53,
116, 123
in strategy choosing, 53, 55, 72–74,
92–93
in transition options, 39–40, 56, 73,
75, 93–94
retention, 3–5, 7n2, 63, 67, 117
road map, 38–40
role models, 17–18, 30, 50–53
in Mason case study, 71
in STEM scholar mentoring
program, 44
in transition to workplace or
graduate studies, 83

SACNAS. *See* Society for Chicanos and
Native Americans in Science
Sanderson, Mark, 1–2, 91–94
scholar mentoring programs, STEM,
44–46, 62
scholar programs, 44–47, 53–55,
62, 120
science, technology, engineering, and
mathematics. *See* STEM
science, technology, engineering, arts
and mathematics. *See* STEAM
Science Posse Scholars Program,
46
self-efficacy, 13, 30, 63, 66
seminars, first-year, xiv, 47, 50,
54, 56
SI. *See supplemental instruction*
social fit, 43

Society for Chicanos and Native
Americans in Science (SACNAS),
84, 121
Society for Women Engineers, 92
spatial visualization skills, 14, 19, 69
speakers. *See* guests and guest speakers
STARS Computing Corps program, 85
STEAM (science, technology,
engineering, arts and
mathematics), 49, 51
Steele, Claude, 110–11
STEM (science, technology,
engineering, and mathematics),
7, 7n1
career, 2–4, 15–17, 52, 66, 82, 84
persistence in, 1, 3, 5–6, 11–12,
44, 63
recruitment, 43–44, 70
scholar mentoring programs,
44–46, 62
student club, 49, 84
transfer students, 3, 39
stereotype threat, 14
students
departmental climate impacting,
50–51, 70–71, 89–91
first-year, 47, 50, 53, 56, 73
STEM, club, 49, 84
students, of color, 64, 125
African American, 21, 36–37
demographics in, 1, 3, 14, 17, 21–22
in Mason case study, 71–72, 74
as Posse scholars, 46
scholars program impacting, 46
students, transfer, 47–48, 51, 71
community college, 1, 21–22,
33, 125
demographics of, 1, 3, 15, 17
in Sanderson case study, 91–93
STEM, 3, 39
studio model, 68
summer bridge programs, 48
summer orientation, 48
summer research program, 36, 61–65
supplemental instruction (SI), 67–68

(Continued from preceding page)

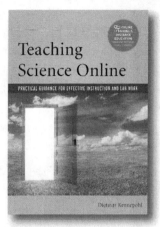

Teaching Science Online
Practical Guidance for Effective Instruction and Lab Work

Edited by Dietmar Kennepohl

With the increasing focus on science education, growing attention is being paid to how science is taught. Educators in science and science-related disciplines are recognizing that distance delivery opens up new opportunities for delivering information; providing interactivity, collaborative opportunities and feedback; and increasing access for students.

This book presents the guidance of expert science educators from the United States and around the globe. They describe key concepts, delivery modes and emerging technologies, and offer models of practice. The book places particular emphasis on experimentation, lab work, and field work as they are fundamentally part of the education in most scientific disciplines.

Coverage includes the following:

- Discipline methodology and teaching strategies in the specific areas of physics, biology, chemistry and earth sciences
- An overview of the important and appropriate learning technologies (ICTs) for each major science
- Best practices for establishing and maintaining a successful course online
- Insights and tips for handling practical components like laboratories and field work
- Coverage of breaking topics, including massive open online courses (MOOCs), learning analytics, open educational resources, and mobile learning
- Strategies for engaging your students online

A companion website presents videos of the contributors sharing additional guidance, virtual labs simulations and various additional resources.

22883 Quicksilver Drive
Sterling, VA 20166-2102   Subscribe to our e-mail alerts: www.Styluspub.com

Also available from Stylus

Teaching Undergraduate Science
A Guide to Overcoming Obstacles to Student Learning

Linda C. Hodges

Foreword by Jeanne L. Narum

"A very important handbook, I highly recommend it for all STEM faculty. I found the entire book engrossing and very easy to read. I easily saw exciting and new ways to apply it. The chapters combine great summaries of fundamental literature on learning and teaching ("why do it") with great ideas on *how* to do it including key examples from the literature. Powerfully and uniquely focused on the key problems faculty perceive in their classes."—***Craig E. Nelson***, *Professor (Emeritus) & Faculty Development Consultant, Biology & SOTL, Indiana University Bloomington*

"Hodges makes a strong case for approaching issues in the science classroom the same way a scientist conducts research: by understanding the issue, identifying how others have addressed similar situations, becoming familiar with literature in the field, and practicing and applying the available theories and tools. To this end, the book's charts provide useful prompts for personal reflections and communal conversations about integrating new strategies into one's teaching repertoire.

Teaching Undergraduate Science is a valuable reminder of where we are now in understanding how learning happens and how particular learning strategies work to overcome obstacles in the classroom."—***Jeanne L. Narum***, *Director Emeritus, Project Kaleidoscope*

"This book is a must-read for any college science instructor. Hodges summarizes key ideas from a wide variety of educational research to highlight the most important barriers to student learning in college science courses. She then connects these ideas to a range of actionable instructional techniques. Each instructional technique is rated in terms of time and effort required to implement. This is an impressive synthesis of practical ideas written with minimal jargon."—***Charles Henderson***, *Professor, Department of Physics and Director, Mallinson Institute for Science Education, Western Michigan University*

(Continues on previous page)